Gathering with friends and family JENNIFER | Summer swimming in the lake MELISSA | Reading on the beach RACHEL | Girls' trip with my besties KATIE | Laughing with family and friends NATALIE | Fresh corn on the cob MELISSA | Watching the sunrise ABBY | Playing games with my grandkids TRUDY | Browsing HomeGoods with coffee LYNN | Family dance party, endless giggles HALEY | Helping others succeed TRUDY | Breakfast date with friends ALYSSA | Last-minute plane tickets LORI | Mom & me on the porch MOLLY | Running half-marathons in each state JENNIFER | Visit son in Paraguay, PeaceCorp KIM | Tea/coffee parties on front porch SHERRY | Reading an amazing book fireside AMY | Free time with my hubby SHAWNNA | Kayaking down a lazy river BETHANY | Hanging out with my siblings JOY | Morning walk on the beach STACY | Mountain vacation with friends KAREN | Walking the streets of Paris KELLY | Celebrating Christmas with Jesus SAM | Being in the Smoky Mountains LISA | opera SARAH | Living my best HEALTHY life BRANDI | Telling stories with friends MARILYN | Time with my family RUTHANNE | Traveling with no particular LYN | Walking to dinner with my family AMY | Being Mommy to Baby Uno CHRISSY | Family, friends, football, food, fun TERRY | Beach sunset hammock | Traveling anywhere with my people CARLY | Spending time in nature COLLEEN | Date night with my husband LAUREN | Traveling the world SUSAN | ch friends ANNASTASIA | Hiking with my family MELANIE | Hanging with Abby, Aimee & Connor ABBY | A relaxing afternoon with friends MYA | Cuddling le, Cooper LESLEY | Paddleboarding in ocean with family ANDREA | A night without diapers—100% AMADI | Super fancy date night GRACE | Taking ises CHRISTY | DISNEY WORLD MORGAN | Reading on a beach LAURA | Spending time with my people ANNA | Piano bar with my girls KAYLEE | True and Enneagram KATIE | Being all in for Piper ALEXANDRIA | NYC @ Christmas with girlfriends BETH | Exploring the best local restaurants LEA | Sipping nds EMILYANN | Silence, coffee, and God's Word NOLVIA | Flying ANYWHERE! JESSYE | Time in Destin with family KELLE | Coffee in a | Cabin getaway with friends KATELYN | Girls' weekend in Traverse City SHANNON | Traveling with my husband, Mike ERIN | Zip-line w/ bestie over ILY | Starting a podcast RACHEL | Food, friends, laughter, games CHARMAINE | A dance party with friends LAUREN | Traveling with family and friends GRETCHEN | Sharing a ORGAN | Getting a manicure ALLISON | Baking a cake Great British Baking Show-style TIFFANY | Going to a concert HOLLY | Laughing with my people abbath with my brothers DANIELLA | Shopping for more houseplants EMILY | Hiking by the lake KATE | Visit all the national parks KATIE | Playing JULIE | Long walks by myself SARAH | My feet in warm sand KRISTIN | PJs. Besties. Wine. Cheese. Reminiscing. SHAUNA | San Diego with my people KATIE | Hiking mountains with my husband KERBY | Misty morning campfire by the lake CHRISTINE | Beach time with best friends KRISTIN | Celebrating everything with my people LAUREN | Lake days with my family KATIE | Snuggling with puppies ERICA | Chicago night with my husband LINDY | Being active outside with friends EMILIE | A sister road trip RACHEL | Starting Christmas in late October SANDRA | A good cuppa tea CHRISTINE | Ben Rector Concert in March BAILEY | Quality time with my friends ASHLEY | Ice coffee, husband, book, beach ALI | Family camp at Kanakuk Kamps BRITTANY | Beach day with my dog MICHELLE | Climbing a really tall mountain SARAH | Friendsgiving with my people LINDY | Music. Piano and horn. Alone. JAMIE | National parks with my family GINJ | Finishing my first marathon SARAH | Christmas baking for my people REYCHEL | Greece & Israel with my friends DAWN | Surprise party for my Ma TAYLOR | Nerts with my family JAMI | Watching Netflix & eating pizza LAUREN | Coffee dates with my friends KATHLYN | Exploring national parks with family GINI | Cooking Korean for my friends AMELIA | Loving God & my people LAUREN | Having Bible study with friends NICOLE | Cheering on my baseball teams SUSAN | Spending time with my family ERIN | A cross-country RV trip CAITLYN | Vacation in Italy with family NICOLE | Rock climbing with friends PAIGE | Traditions with my best friends BROOKE | Game night with friends ALLISON | 3OA with MEGAN | An entire day at Dollywood COURTNEY | Road tripping with my family BROOKE | Game night with friends ALLISON | 3OA with my family ERIN | Moving to Alaska next spring ALLIE | NYC at Christmas and NYE VICTORIA | Laughing around the dinner table KELLY | Making quilts with my mom LAURA | Date night with my husband JEANNINE | Crossing the finish line KAITLYN |

D1010652

Exploring the world with friends ASHLEIGH | Being with my favorite people NICOLE | Discovering local coffee shops LAURALEE | Watching football with my boys ERIC | Cozy evenings by the fire JENNIE | Disney+ with my kid BETH | Coffee with friends–hockey SARAH | Road trip with my friends JAMIE | Going to a cat cafe MEGAN | Five words? I need 500 ANNA | Attending a Michigan football game JULIE | Life chats with friends PAUL | Karaoke Christmas party with family RACHEL | Talking to friends about Jesus MACKENZIE | Going to the lake LAUREN | Reading on the beach CRYSTAL | Seeing an Astros baseball game LAURA | Going to ballet class CELENIA | Reading on Gatlinburg cabin porch ROBIN | Creating something beautiful and comforting BONNIE | Games and food with anyone KAREN | Snuggling with my sweet baby ASHLEE | Waterskiing & being on the water KENDRA | Traveling with my mom AUDREY | Tea with a friend TESSA | Swimming with dolphins in Bermuda ROBIN | Camping adventures with my family CHERYL | Hiking with my favourite friends ROBIN | Saturday morning farmers market EMILY | On the beach ocean watching DENISE | Laughing with my nephews KATIE | Quality time with incredible friends LANEE | Seeing a musical with friends AMY | Seeing the Colosseum AMY | Beach. Books. Sunshine. Family. Friends. KATIE | Tuesday night watercolor classes STEPHANIE | Good coffee and great conversation SARAH | Caribbean vacay with my fam HEATHER | Scotland with my handsome man SARAH | Weekend trip with my hubby JEN | Beach sitting ALL DAY LONG MELINDA | Walking at Radnor with friends CHRISTY | Watching Hallmark Christmas movies JENA | A London trip with Gabs SARAH | Being home for Christmas ABIGAYLE | Themed charcuterie board with friends JANET | Jesus. Broadway. Sunrise. Coffee. Lake. COREY | Reading on a rainy-day KELLY | Visiting all fifty state capitals MEG | Eating ice cream with friends HANNAH | Reading books at the beach CARI | Being with my people LEAH | Hiking with my family HEIDI | schedule-free week away ERICA | Disney World with my family BROOKE | Biking in Berlin with friends KATIE | Traveling to Paris with family MADDIE | A Cocoa under the Christmas tree NIKKI | Exploring a new city PAIGE | Balloon ride with my husband ERICA | Wandering around taking photos TERESA | Backpacking through Europe sounds fun NIKKI | Getting to play tuba again JACOB | A free vacation to Spain LAUREN | Fishing the flats with Josh SYDNEY | A week in Paris AIMEE | Thanksgiving at beach w/ friends & mimosas KASIE | Puns. Gnomes. Sunrise. Queso. Auntie. LISA MARIE | Birth of my first grandchild AMY | Sunsets, fireworks, good food, friends DIANA | Hiking all over the world CHELSEA | Playing with my kindergarten students KIMMY | Good coffee and great conversations EMILY | Cuddles with my kids JODI | Disneyland with my husband SARAH | New cities with old friends JESSICA | Sewing all day long JEANETTE | Watching The Crown LYDIA | European vacation with my husband JOY | I am enjoying HOT yoga ANGELA | Watching the sunset with friends KELSEY | Snuggles with my people SUZI | Sunday afternoon naps KEZIA | Serving kids at Transformation Church ERIKA | Disney World. Always Disney World. JULIANNE | Becoming a family of three TAYLOR | Going to Disneyland with family LOUISE | Creating memories with our Lukebug SWEENA | Going to Disneyland with Carrissa DARCY | Colorado with my husband ARIE | Backpacking in Yosemite with friends LEGARE | Visiting my sponsored child HILARY | Cry-laughing, family & promises fulfilled LYDIA | Puzzles, hot chocolate, a fire REBECCA | Reading books at the beach AMBER | Unplugged vacation with my family KAYLAN | Spending time with my nephews CAMERON | A long run and brunch LIZ | Going to Hawaii JULIA | Having a classic movies marathon SARAH | Road tripping with my husband SAMANTHA | Disney+ and Blue Bell MORGAN | Traveling, reading, cooking, journaling & husband STEPHANIE | Reading books in my hammock APRIL | A grown-up field day BECKY | Girls' trip to Paris JILL | The Oz Dust Ballroom EBERT | Quality time with my people CHRISTINA | Dinner out with a friend LACEY | Wes, Nathan, Daniel, me, vacation EMILY | Snuggling with my sweet daughter RACHEL | Traveling somewhere with great snorkeling EMILY | Eat all of the food DANIELLE | Dancing for God under trees ELITA | Being lake and loved ones SHELBI | Being with Galen and Cooper KAITLYN | Lazy Saturdays with my family KATIE | Going to Zumba with friends STACIE | Road trip with my friends JAMIE | ERIN | Road trip with my friends JAMIE |

who God made me TRACY | Music–listen, sing, and play DAVE | Belly laughing with old friends AMY | The Road trips with my sister JEN | Loving Chase and our Noah WHITNEY | A girls' night SHELLEY | Traveling Being with my family ANNA | Coast to coast road trip JORDAN | Starting a family NIKKI | Beach house with my people KATIE | Browsing bookshops with a mocha JESSICA | Being with my people KATIE | Family walks JENI | Book, fire, blanket, and coffee NOELLE | Learning to play piano again my family ELIZABETH | Browsing bookshops CHRISTINA | Visiting all US National Parks KIMBERLY | Time with my nieces & nephew CHRISTINA |

GEORGIA

[...]pa with girlfriends, wine, cheese NIKI | Travel the world with friends MENDY | College

[...]people involved AMY | Piloting a biplane and hang gliding SARA | Singing with lifelong friends JENI | Days

[...]friends REBECCA | Traveling the world for one year ALISON | Future travels when we're married CARA | Traveling. Reading. Beach.

daughter and husband ASHLEY | Eating food and loving people LEAH | Mentoring teen girls JENNEE | A fun family trip WHITNEY | Long drives listening to podcasts ANDREA | A trip around the WORLD

church TYLER | Snuggles with my newest baby MONICA | Being crowned queen of birthdays HOLLY | Puppies, flowers, sunshine, laughing, confetti CAITLYN | Time with

LISA | Full house, food, family, friends HOLLY | Doing LIFE with my Eddie BROOKE | Summer vacation in Avalon, NJ AMANDA | Being with my favorite people ABBEY

GRACE | Seeing my parents be grandparents BRITTANY | Wine night with my girls JULIE | MiniBFF time MEL | Hiking a new trail MEG. | Traveling across the country

JAMIE | Girls' trip with my friends JASMINE | Beach vacation with my husband AMBER | Gelato in Rome with BFFs KATIE | Eating pizza in bed KAITLIN | Disney with my

husband JENNIFER | Road trip with family BETSY | Witnessing my ohana experience JOY KIM | Trip to Maine in fall SARAH | A second honeymoon to Europe JORDAN |

Beach, golden retrievers, husband, mai tai KATE | Reading books with a cappuccino JENA | Reading a book after sleeping in KRISTIN | Watching an incredible

documentary ANNA | Camping & soccer with son NATE | Quiet coffee with a view BEKAH | Christmas in New York City EMILY | Vanilla chai at Ebenezer's CALLIE |

Curling up by a fire ABBY | Learning something new MARY | Ireland with my whole family JENICE | Vacay in New York GABY | No-smartphone family game weekend

SUSAN | Reading at the beach RACHEL | Saturday morning runs with Mark MARCIE | Hiking to beautiful waterfalls SAM | Kicking through fall leaves AMY | Traveling

with my family POLLY | Window-shopping with iced coffee JORDAN | Baking with my grandchildren CATHY | Tea & a good book LISA | Leading Young Life with my

husband EMILY | Getting bubble tea with friends RILLIAN | Heading out to the lake ALI | Weeklong family beach vacation CRYSTAL | Riding horses with my friends

MEREDITH | Reading on a rainy day CAITLIN | Tex-Mex patio dinner with friends PAIGE | Playing pranks on my husband BRE | Kayaking with my nephews EVONNA |

Watching sunsets at the beach BRITTANY | Spending time with people LAURA | Riding bikes along the beach ROXANN | Going to Disney World RACHEL | Strolling around

a botanical garden JILLAINE | Deboarding airplane, passport in hand CAITLIN | Escape room with friends COURTNEY | Going for a run JACKIE | Traveling with friends

HEATHER | Seeing an Oscar movie together MICHAEL | Tweedling with my best friend MARIANNE | Thru-hiking the Appalachian Trail CINDY | Traveling and exploring the

world KYLIE | Wine and cheese with friends KAELYN | Watching Alabama football in Tuscaloosa LAURA | Doing crafts with my niece RENEE | Baking day with friends

KAYLI | Spending quality time with friends NATALIE | Christmas. Campfires. Scooters. Beach trips. KAYLA | Annual sisters' weekends since 2006 AMY | Alone time and

Sonic tea SARAH | BFF, me, NYC bookstore crawl MICHELE | Cooking for special family meals CINDY | Riding bike at the beach DONNA | Going hiking with my family

ANDREA | Having a kitchen dance party OLIVIA | Beaches, family, books, friends, cooking CATHRYN | Going to the beach ROXANNE | Cuddling with my adorable baby

LEANNA | Spending time with my boys PAM | Travel without fears or hesitations STACEY | Christmas lights & Hallmark movies LIV | Going on a hike JESSICA | Meeting

Dansby at SunTrust JILL | Going on an Alaskan cruise SUSIE | Watching @lydiataylorr dance SUSIE | Coffee with Kayla AUBREY | Snowy day and chai lattes SOFIA |

Coffee with friends BRITTANY | Cheering on MK next weekend KRISTYN | Laughing about life with others GINNY | A book on the beach COURTNEY | Trying a new

recipe ALLEA | Fabulous forty-year friends podcast JULEE | Being with all my people MELISSA | Being called Aunt Banana ANNA MCCOLLUM | Themed dinner party

with friends ANNE | Having friends over for dinner GABY | A relaxing hot bath LIZZIE | Dinner and theatre with girlfriends NICKY | Time with my adult daughters JEN |

Paddleboarding with my people KATIE | Running a full marathon KAT | Spa day with girlfriends MARY GRACE | Swimming on a sunny day KYLIE | Assisting in a heart

surgery EMILY | Wine tasting with best friends MEL | Traveling with my husband ANABEL | Coffee, friends, cake, and chatting BRITTANY |

Foodie tour across Europe ALEXIS | Having a baby TAYLOR | Big house, friends, food, laughter JESSIE | Roller skating with my people MK | Teaching and loving little ones HAILEY | Traveling ANYWHERE w/ friends & food ANGEL | Being with my people ALLIE | Books and coffee in bed RACHEL | Spending time with my girls WALTER | Decorating for Christmas LAUREN | Spending time with my family KAREN | Beach vacations and doggie cuddles KIRSTIE | Trying a new restaurant AMY | Movies and pizza with friends RACHAEL | A day at the spa AMANDA | Watching A&M beat Georgia AMY | A Saturday spent baking KATHLEEN | Husband, friends, food, movies, music LEANNA | Whale watching CAITY | Hiking in Arches National Park MARCIE | Moving my family to Europe ASHELYN | Hiking in spring and fall BRANDON | The beach with my people HOLLY | England with my best friend KRISTIN | Being with my sisters GRETCHEN | Road trip with my Mama JESSIE | Hammock + book + Lake Cumberland KATY | Sitting by a fire RUTH | Building in my woodworking shop SAMANTHA | My puppies and my people HOLLY | Adopting a second child DEBORAH | Loud laughter and comfortable silences KAT | Tractor rides with my husband BROOKE | Anything at a peaceful pace ROSA | Traveling somewhere new LINDSEY | Coffee with Aunt Nicole LEANDRA | Baking cookies JENNIFER | Beach days and traveling with friends CHELSEA | Reading, crafting, podcast KATELYN | Friends, coffee, nature, and laughter MEGAN | Spoiling my nephews JODI | Singing a song with Patrick SARAH | Spending time with my family JAMIE | Dinner party with loved ones SARAH | Using my gift of music LILLA | Game night with old friends AUDREY | Traveling with friends and family KATIE | Mimi moments with my grandchildren PHYLLIS | Hiking with my people STACI | Worshipping at The Bridge Church JENNA | Spending time with our granddaughter KATHRYN | Snowshoe/ mobile in the Rockies KELSEY | Exploring new places with friends SARAH | Meeting my son—May 2020 MELO | The beach with friends SARA | Vacation with my family KRISTY | Coffee, blanket & Annie's podcast KAREN | Friends, TV, and my dog JULIE | Yummy coffee around the world TAYLOR | Quality time with my people AUDREY | MEGAN | Rooftop dance party with BFFs MOLLY | Beach vacation with family + friends LAUREN | Holding my future babies CINDY | For Jesus to come back AUDREY | Playing the NY Times crossword MOLLY | Knitting sweaters while watching Gilmore Girls SHERRY | Traveling with my family BROOKE | Seaside sunset watching KRISTEN | Traveling with my husband, Jorge MACKENZIE | Spending time with family EMILY | Late night wine with family KATE | Exploring Greece & South America JANIE | Coffee. Friends. Laughter. Window shopping. ABBY | Laughing so hard I cry. KARA | Spending $20,000 in one day KELSEY | Going to Disneyland BRITTANY | Bougie breakfast dates with hubby CINDY | Watching my girls play sports AMY | Wine & girlfriends around a fire. MELISSA | Dreaming ... ALEXA | Paddleboarding on the lake JANIE | Hot stone massage, YES LORD MACKENZIE | Shopping the clearance at Target KATIE | ... Knitting with Knit Club Ladies MITZI | Hot chocolate and Christmas movies JESSICA | Talks, walks, laughing, bubbles, kites ... skipping stones & blowing bubbles SISSY | Waterskiing at sunrise with family HALEY | Travel. Explore with family, friends. ... Going to London in January ANNA | Laughing until my stomach hurts JESSI | Recording music with my friends ... with my family BRANDY | Coffee date with a friend JULIA | Playing with my dog TAYLOR | Friends bonfire ... ...-hopping with fam LYDIA | Spending time with my family DANA | Riding roller coasters at ... ...NNA | Reading with warm tea CARRIE | Breakfast with my favorite people SARAH | Hiking ...saw puzzles JALEESA | Kitchen dancing with my husband SARAH | Hiking ... ... East Coast road trip AMANDA | Running a marathon LEXIE | ... ...-king West Virginia with family EMILY | Relaxing with ... ... ...-ting, friends, baking, hiking, books HILARY | ... ... ...-with friends BARB | Adventuring with ... ... ...-ing, friends, family AMBER |

Disneyland with my family JILL | Marrying my best friend, Justin JORDAN | N...
football Saturday with family SCOTT | Anything with my ...
spent at the lake AMY | Brunch with f...
Coffeehouse O...

# That Sounds Fun

Coffee with my best friend MIKAYLA | Traveling the world with family LIESL | Holding a baby chimp LORI | Nurse friends drinking wine together SARAH | Skiing down a majestic snowy mountain PAM | Hugging my mini donkeys ASHLEY | Traveling the US and writing ALEYAH | Going to the beach RUTH | 90s dance party JEN | Trampoline exercise class to music AMANDA | Jumping on trampolines AMANDA | Playing in Walt Disney World CAROLYN | Sewing quilts for loved ones ANNE | Being with my people CARRIE | ManU game @ Old Trafford MELISSA | To meet you over coffee EMMA | Book, blanket, coffee KARLA | Exploring national parks SARAH | Wine, cheese, friends KARLA | Connecting with others through photography ANNA | Long bath on rainy day TARA | Meeting believers at craft shows BRITTNEY | Time with my people RACHEL | Watching elephants in Lake Kariba STACEY | Game nights with my friends ABBY | Toddler toots and belly laughs SARAH | Spending time with Gramercy Hope RACHEL | Going to country concerts :) JORDAN | Unlimited Starbucks in the beach BETHANY | Tubing down our farm rapids STACEY | Office supply shopping HEATHER | Friends & food around the table HOPE | Snorkeling. Reading. Painting. Kayaking. SLEEPING. LAURA | Watching Hallmark movies with my kitties JESSIE | Traveling with my wife JEFF | Swimming with dolphins in Mauritius STACEY | Watching football with my family SHELBY | Combine rides with Dad ELIZABETH | Snow skiing with my husband JESSICA | Hosting dinner parties for friends KATIE | Enjoying the Texas Hill Country CHASITY | Chasing Luca and Jack TIFFANY | Chasing dreams with my family AMANDA | Long slow walks on beach AMY | Dear ones gather around table LEANNE | Concerts with my wife BEN | Family trip to Hawaii KRISTA | Farm-to-table dinner at sunset JEN | Global ice cream tasting tour LEIGH ANN | Puzzling with my best friends CLAIRE | A Murder, She Wrote marathon RACHEL | Horseback riding ASHLEY | Running beside a trickling stream KAELA | Travel, family, food, sunrises SARAH | Eating food and doing karaoke CAILYN | Playing songs on instruments COLIN | Kittens—lots of kittens LEE | Playing with LEGOs LIAM | Derby match at Old Trafford BILL | Mountain biking in crisp weather POLINA | Reading by the fireplace RACHEL | A girls' trip to Nashville JONI | Vacation with my new family EMILY | Windows down, music up ALI | Laughing with my boys STEPHANIE | Ice-skating party with friends ABIGAIL JOY | Quality time with my bestie(s) WALLY | Starting and growing my business CHERYL | Playing with LEGOs LIAM | A long walk on beach LAUREL | Living on a goat farm JENNA | Surfing and yoga TAYLOR | Good book & afternoon nap BETH | Hiking with my ups EMMA | A trip to Alaska SARAH | Paddleboarding in the ocean BECKIE | Traveling abroad with incredible friends CARLY | Best friends beach trip MEGAN | Hot Vinyasa yoga before cocktails PATIENCE | Walking barefoot in the grass ERIN | A vat of healthy chocolate KIM | Chasing waterfalls around the nation TYLER | Finding new local coffee shops BETHANY | Creating fun resources for families AMANDA | Auburn football with my hubby MARISSA | Sharing a table with friends TAYLOR | Pretty much anything with Heather REBECCA | A beach vacation ALAINA | Reading a good book KATIE | Celebrating the Christmas season BETH | Road trips with my husband SHELLEY | Time Entertaining people in my home CASEY | Long conversations with old friends JESSICA | Strolling by the Eno River OLIVIA | A good restaurant with family HOLLY | Time with friends and family LISA | Scooter scavenger hunt w/ BFFs LISA | Making pumpkin pie with family KRYSTLE | Launching a person or idea TIFFANY | Floating on the lake AUTUMN | Long walk on the beach ANNE | Sound of Music bike tour LILY | Picnicking on an autumn day KAREN | Traveling with my friends CALLIE | Kentucky basketball winning another championship SARAH | Family hiking in the mountains LISA | Being FOR the next generation ALICIA | Cross-country road trip AMBER | Shopping with my daughters VICKI | Mountains. College friends. Togetherness. Laughter. STEPHANIE | Good coffee with good friends CHRISSY | A day on the water KELLIE | Traveling with mom and aunt KELSEY | Playing soccer anywhere, anytime ADDISON | A movie marathon snow day PAIGE | Charcuterie board and Mumm champagne NICHOLE | Road trip with my family BRITTANY | Seeing a sky full of stars ELIZABETH | Dark chocolate and red wine BETO | Enjoying the Texas Hill Country CHASITY | Cooking good food for friends ASHLEY | Road tripping with friends KAILYN | Reading, relationships, grandkids, bubble tea KATHY | Teaching 6-year-olds TAYLOR | Singing in a modern choir KATE | Being a backup singer MEGAN | Gathering with family and friends JESS | Reading on the beach MEGAN | Graduating nursing school CASSEY | Lord of the Rings marathon MICHELLE | Running with my sister Lisa DANA | Vacation with family CHERI | Working with my 5th graders BOBBI | Singing in the street SAM | Sipping tea in Ireland MCKENZIE | Traveling with my husband/family KARLY | Florida Gators football game KATIE | Hiking in the rain ABIGAIL |

# That Sounds Fun

## THE JOYS OF BEING AN AMATEUR,
## THE POWER OF FALLING IN LOVE,
## AND WHY YOU NEED A HOBBY

# Annie F. Downs

**Revell**

a division of Baker Publishing Group
Grand Rapids, Michigan

© 2021 by Annie F. Downs

Published by Revell
a division of Baker Publishing Group
PO Box 6287, Grand Rapids, MI 49516-6287
www.revellbooks.com

Printed in the United States of America

Library of Congress Cataloging-in-Publication Data
Names: Downs, Annie F., 1980- author.
Title: That sounds fun : the joys of being an amateur, the power of falling in
    love, and why you need a hobby / Annie F. Downs.
Description: Grand Rapids, Michigan : Revell, a division of Baker Publishing
    Group, 2021.
Identifiers: LCCN 2020024913 | ISBN 9780800738747 (cloth)
Subjects: LCSH: Amusements—Religious aspects—Christianity. | Play—
    Religious aspects—Christianity. | Hobbies—Religious aspects—Christianity.
    | Christian life. | Christianity and culture.
Classification: LCC BV4597 .D69 2021 | DDC 248.4/6—dc23
LC record available at https://lccn.loc.gov/2020024913
ISBN 978-0-8007-4030-6 (ITPE)

The author is represented by Alive Literary Agency, www.aliveliterary.com.

Interior design by William Overbeeke.

21   22   23   24   25   26   27       7   6   5   4   3   2   1

To the *That Sounds Fun* podcast listeners.
You show up, you love our guest friends so well,
and you always remind me that
what we are making matters.
You taught me, and continue to teach me,
how to chase the fun,
knowing I won't be alone when I find it.
Thank you.

Laying on grass with friends TORI | Boating with friends & family JULIE | Ice skating or swing dancing KAYLEA | Making a positive difference every day RICHIE | Clean comedy show with family NICOLE | Hiking with my friends LESLIE | Lattes and deep chats CONNIE | Kayaking with my sister Sue PENNY | Tubing the river with framily NICOLE | Watching grown sons play together MARCIA | Night away with my hubster KAROLINE | Face-to-face time with my people ANNE | Crocheting and meeting new friends ALYSSA | Community, creativity, friends, and obviously, food MACKENZIE | Laughing with the grandkids JANET | Family trips JANET | Jeeping in the mountains ALEXIS | Meeting friends at Five80 Coffeehouse CHLOE | Coffee, friends, worship, laughter, Oreos AUDREY | Dance party with grandkids JANET | Walking down Main Street in Disney MARYCOLE | Playing soccer with my son AUSTIN | Going on a beach picnic CLAUDIA | Going to the Holy Land THOMPSON | Campfire under the stars TIFFANY | Serving Jesus's Bride locally GRACIE | Hanging out with my niece SIERRA | Road trips with best friends KATIE | Saturday morning breakfast out ANNE | Disney World at Christmas MELISSA | Pet an elephant KENNEDY | Warm sun. Bible open. Listening. CRYSTAL | Spending uninterrupted time with friends ALLY | Date night with my husband DANIELLE | Visit all major zoos LIZZY | The beach with my people JESSICA | Impromptu patio parties MELISSA | Walk beach with whole family LAURALEE | Having a Harry Potter marathon LYDIA | Taking long, hot baths KIMBERLY | Family vacations on Sanibel Island LYNNE | Hallmark movies and Christmas cookies AMY | Laughing with my friends JENNIFER | Going to a country concert KATIE | Being with my family ESTHER | Taking a nap KRISTIN | Vacation in California with family SANDY | Adventures with awesome friends MADISON | Climbing and soccer with friends MORGAN | Visiting Disney World with family JULIA | Watching African sunsets with friends ROSIE | Dancing in raining confetti BREE | Travel to Disney with family HEATHER | Hot bath and celebrity magazine MONICA | Card games with friends ARIEL | Being debt free in 2020 BECKY | Young Life camp LESLIE | Time Laughing with my coworkers AMANDA | Adventures with my husband JOHN | A good game of rugby KYLE | Taking a cross-country road trip EMILY | A sleepover in a castle KATELYN | Adventures with my kids & wife JOHN | Making sandcastles with grandsons ANGIE | A tea party with friends KERRY | Sleeping, rain, reading, music & friends SARAH | Wine on veranda at the beach CAROL | S'mores brownies. Reading. Dancing. LYNN | Road tripping coast to coast ARIEL | Doing photography for a living HEATHER | Adventures with friends ALICIA | A cruise with my family JULIE | Beach with my five boys KASSY | The beach and friends JORDAN | Loving JW and Mary Mac BETH | Disneyland at night with friends JESSICA | Hiking mountains with my family JOY | Time with my new husband MOLLY | Pajama day with my family NICOLE | Tea, crochet, fireplace, Christmas movies AMANDA | Doing crafts with my daughters KATE | Road trip with my girlfriends BILLIE JO | Visiting Pacific Northwest with Glen LYNDSEY | Family game night ERIN | Sleeping—infant/toddler mom life CHELSEA | Snuggling with my two cats ASHLEY | Baking cookies and eating them RACHEL | PEACE at the beach JULI | Time alone with my husband STEPHANIE | Renovating our old farmhouse ERIN | All my people laughing together ABBY | Baking for my friends ASHLIN | Going hiking BETH-ANNE | Eating new foods with family REBECCA | Watching Astros baseball with Josh KALAN | Hiking on a sunny day KRISTIN | Hot cocoa by the fire CHRIS | Trips with friends and family ANDREA | Reading while watching the rain CULLEN | Eating tropical fruit in Hawaii LEORA | Cooking BBQ for friends & family BRENT | Photographing wildlife in Yellowstone REBEKAH | Visiting all the MLB parks DENISE | A weekend in the mountains KATIE | Hanging with my kids Hiking with my children ROBYN | & grandchildren LINDA | Running with dogs & baby CAREY | Improving processes for FedEx SARAH | Snuggling Sipping coffee with my friends EMILYANN | Exploring God's glory JULES | A weekend with college girlfriends REBECCA | Going on a my people drinking coffee ASHLEY | Serving with my family MARIA | Camping in the Adirondack Mountains LIZ | World traveling picnic BECCA | Being a mirror of Truth SHERRI | Cooking and eating with family CATALINA | A day at the beach KERA | World traveling with my husband SARAH | Hanging with Carter and Grace BUNNI | Healing, growing, and feeling alive EMMALEE | Hiking with my husband JENNIFER | Living fearless and free ANNA | Enjoy Christmas music before Thanksgiving KAMI | Going to a Broadway show LIZ | Adventure with people I love CAROLINE | Photographing people's extraordinary lives TIM | Drinking tea in a tree NADIA | Family river adventure time ALYSSA | Time at home being creative JULIANNE | Shopping for a great deal EMILY | Traveling with husband and daughter ASHLEY |

# Contents

## WHY YOU NEED A HOBBY

## CHASE THE FUN

# Hello

Hi friends.

Welcome to a very special episode of *That Sounds Fun*. I'm your host, Annie F. Downs, and I'm so happy to be here with you today.

This is a little different from the normal episodes we share, as this conversation is a whole book instead of a one-hour sit-down between two friends that you can listen to as you walk or drive or work or play.

But my hope is the same. My hope is that you feel like you are sitting at the table with me or that we are out on a walk together or that I'm a fellow passenger on your commute to work, or that I'm on the treadmill beside you as we dig deeper into this little word. F—U—N. Fun. How to find it, what it looks like, and why you long for it. And maybe, just maybe, by the end of this time together we'll both be a bit different, a bit lighter, and a bit more understanding toward ourselves and each other.

By the way, throughout the book you will see pages of small font turned sideways (as a matter of fact, you've already passed a few of them!). When I asked my podcast listeners to tell me what sounded fun to them, these were their answers!

Relaxing with friends and family HEATHER | Seeing *Hamilton* on Broadway LAUREN | Hanging with #myfavoritetinyhuman KATIE | SKIING especially with fresh powder DONNA | Going on a mission trip DARCI | Front porch swing talks JOHN | Rainy days and riveting reads SAVANNAH | Good food with friends/family SHEREE | Swimming in sun with COKE-ICEE KAYLA | 12South, Ryman, Frothy, Craft South, Athenian JESSICA | Books and movies and friends KAREN | Date night with my husband LINDSAY | Traveling and exploring new places CATLYN | Baylor football wins national championship RANDAL | Getting my Masters in MFT RILEY | Trip across America with teenagers DALLAS | Photographing wildlife in Yellowstone REBEKAH | Go on cruise with husband ALICIA | Becoming "Mom" via matched adoption BONNIE | Traveling the world with friends DARCY | Watching Hallmark with cold champagne KIMMY | Hearing my grandchildren laugh BETH | Baking cupcakes KIM | Having more babies KATIE | Eating at Cookout with Makaylah FAITH | Baking Christmas cookies SARA | Going to Disneyland with friends AMANDA | Traveling the entire world SAMANTHA | Medical mission trip ALLIE | Going for a run KATELYN | Time with my nieces/nephews LISA | Golfing on a sunny day ASHLEE | Pod-bath with a face mask CAROLINE | Friend and miniBFF time ASHTON | Surprise party for my Ma TAYLOR | Relaxing with my husband KRISTEN | Family, friends, wine, charcuterie table ALISON | Baking and dancing to music SARAH | Watching my babies grow TRACI | Adventuring with family and friends ALLISON | Allllll of the musicals STEPH | Mountain getaway with friends LINDSEYBETH | Coffee time with friends VALERIE | Reading, eating, creating, and worshiping STELLA | Going down waterslides HEATHER | Painting ALICIA | Traveling to Paris bookish life BETH | Laughing with people I love DORIE | Spending Christmas with my family LYDIA | Reading in my cozy bed KRYSTA | Laughing so hard I cry KATE | Phoneless with friends VAL | All-inclusive resort in Mexico SAMANTHA | Hiking in the mountains ABBEY | Disney Springs Starbucks outdoor seating CAROL | Going to Disney with family NATALIE | Reading in bed, all day ASHLEY | Getting locked overnight in Target PATTY | Bonfire with my home team RHIANNON | Laughing with my fiancé CINDY | Healthy, stimulating conversations with friends HAILEY | (Gifted) spa vacation with friends MARTY | Standing-room only concert tickets SHELBY | Catching up with college friends KIRSTEN | Hot tub while it's snowing CASSI | Exploring coffee shops with friends BRITTANY | Exploring a new city with friends ELISE | Friend time AMY | Reading books and watching movies JESSICA | Traveling somewhere new. With coffee. ALYSSA | Adventuring in the mountains COURTNEY | Adventures with my kids HEIDI | God. Friends. Beach. Food. Tea. MARSHA | Hiking in the mountains AMANDA | World travel with my tribe EMILY | Making life moments matter globally LAUREN | Going on my honeymoon MADISON | Introverting with crafts, coffee, chocolate TRACY | Traveling, connecting with my people AMANDA | Camping with husband and dogs BRANDI | Jump into a hidden lake SHERRI | Making memories with my people REBECCA | Exploring countries with my husband LAUREN | Cooking with my best friend RACHAEL | Riding horses with my daughters CALLIE | Playing "Spicy Uno" with friends ALLIE | Charcuterie boards and Monopoly Deal MARIA | Camping with family and friends RACHAEL | Marionberry crisp and ice cream STEPHANIE | Front seat rollercoaster ride giggles ALICIA | Cruise with my best friends DONNA | Swimming in Lake Michigan KATIE | Swinging on any beach JACKIE | Going thrifting with my mom SARAH | Acting on stage ABBY | Get a back massage GREER | Snorkeling DANIELLE | Going hiking in the Rockies MEGAN | Front porch sitting Mandeville, LA LISA | Laughing with friends RENEE | "Race-cation" trips with friends MARGARET | Watching my grandson grow DONNA | Adventures with my sweet man CARA | Game night with my family TANNA | Playing dress up with my daughter ADRIAN | A cool, quiet morning run RACHEL | Hanging with my son, Cole CHRISTIE | Going to Disney World BETH | Snuggling my baby, Winn SUSAN | A massage in Baños, Ecuador SARAH | Monday nights with my Dgroup KELLY | Traveling the world JOY | All-inclusive trip KELLY | Seeing my doggy after vacation :) LUISA | Playing Shakespeare in London REBECKA | Resting and reading SARAH | Going to the beach TREY | Camping at Yosemite WENDY | Traveling around the world JENN | Big libraries; big coffee HANNAH | Spending the day on Lake George, NY LAUREN | Going to shows on Broadway ANGIE | Jesus. Coffee. Running. Candles. Football. KAYLA | Pie, coffee, and long conversation ALLISON | Watching my baby girl learn SAM | Food, Friends, Family = FUN JESSICA | Reading on a rainy day BRUCE | Disney movie marathon RACHEL | Friends connecting over food LARA |

# What Sounds Fun *to* You?

# East Pole Coffee Company

IT'S FALL, and I'm grounded from flying and traveling for work for a few months. By choice. By invitation from God. Though I'm not sure what I think about that.

Over the last seven years of this career, I have racked up miles in the air like a professional, which, according to my status with Delta, I pretty much am. I love to travel. I love seeing places and being places. I love flying.

Travel has always been one of the best parts of my job. But about a year ago, I felt God whisper to me, "You're going to want to be home next fall." It felt like an invitation from Him, and with time in prayer, for me and my team of employees and managers and agents, we decided that I would spend fall in Nashville. What? Fall is my busiest time of year—conferences and events typically keep my travel schedule fully booked in autumn. And God wanted me off the road?

But I heard what I heard and I agreed to obey. And so as I write these words, here I am: grounded.

For a change of scenery, I drove south from Nashville to see my family and I'm posted up at my favorite Atlanta coffee spot: East Pole Coffee Company. It's bright and beautiful, and it looks like it seats about thirty people. In the corners, there are green plants hanging from the ceiling, and the vines are dangling down to the floor, almost camouflaging the electrical outlets. The coffee bar is made of a long and dark maple, and there are these really lovely scalloped white tiles climbing from the white floors to the bar.

I'm sitting with my back to the windows. I like the hubbub of a busy coffee shop, and this one has constant traffic. Also, across the room at a little table for two are my cousin and his wife, who are home from abroad for just a few weeks. I like being able to see them in the same space.

I have a chai with oat milk (which, come on, milk made of oats is ridiculous and hilarious and so bougie but also delicious). The playlist I found on Spotify is a collection of instrumental classics called "refreshing pieces," and I'm switching between it and Jon McLaughlin's instrumental music. Still, all I want to do is slam my computer shut and escape. As I was driving here, my mind started dreaming of all the places I could run to and drive to and fly to and be right now. All the other places but HERE. But if there's one thing I've learned, it's that even if I did run away, there is no getting away from my insides. It's as if the sadness has taken residence, and it's not going to be left behind just because I leave.

And leaving isn't an option right now anyway. I've stopped traveling for work for a couple of reasons, one of them being my physical health. A few months ago, I started getting migraines on almost a daily basis, and I was almost guaranteed to get one every time I flew on a plane. After months of this, my doctor put me on bed rest. Two full weeks of bed rest.

The decision to take the second half of the year off the road was sealed before I started getting daily migraines, but God knew. He knew before I did that the winter would be the winter of migraines and that a full fall calendar probably would have continued to feel invasive. While my body and heart would have been up for it, I worry my brain would not have. But there's lots more to this season off the road. I know there is.

At the start of this season, my friend Matt asked me how I was feeling about being grounded. Matt and I have similar personalities and he told me, "Don't be surprised by a sense of mild depression in this season." WHAT? THAT IS NOT WHAT I WANTED TO HEAR. But even his short message whispered something to me that I haven't been able to ignore. It amplified the chorus that had been singing in the background of my brain for the last few months, leading up to the season of no travel, so quiet it was barely audible. But when someone else called out the lyrics, I heard them clearly: There is something scary to me about months at home without anywhere to go. I haven't done this in almost a decade—been in my own house every night of the week for a lot of weeks.

Fast-forward to spring 2020. If I had only known that just a few months later, we would all learn what it would be like to spend endless amounts of time in our own homes as we collectively experienced the beginning stages of the COVID-19 pandemic, the first global pandemic of our lifetime. Everyone at home. No one in school or church. Most professionals no longer going into the office but working from guest rooms and couches and dining room tables. Some friends of mine thrived; some did not. We began to ask big questions of our world but also big questions about ourselves.

What happens to me when I can't go? When I can't get away from here?

Truth? I wish I were flying away right now. This has been a tough year. It included migraines and heartbreak and quarantine and really hard decisions. And as I think about all those things, something makes me feel like being in a different city would feel better. (It wouldn't. I've done this—tried to fix my problems by hopping on a plane—enough times before. But the whisper is still there. *Run from this and you will feel better.* But I won't feel better. I never do.)

How often do we call escapism "fun"? That's the real question for me. When I'm looking to define fun in my own life, to figure out how to handle the thing I don't know how to handle or how to process the pain I don't know what to do with, I wonder if I'm actually planning fun or just using fun to describe running away.

Today, I want to run. I'll pack a bag with my stuff and a bag with my feelings, then I'll leave the feelings bag behind, grab the other one, and board a plane that will fly me somewhere.

Anywhere.

I FEEL LIKE I'm a good person to tell you about fun and to tell you why you absolutely need fun in your life. For those who don't know, I am the host of a podcast called *That Sounds Fun*. Episodes release twice a week, Mondays and

Thursdays, and in every episode, I get to interview a friend or someone I wish I were friends with. Sometimes they are authors or musicians, and other times they are chefs or athletes or actresses or doctors or anyone who says something I think my listener friends will love.

Because we do need fun. We all have to find it. My friend Emily P. Freeman and I will often tell each other to "chase the fun." Whether your life looks exactly the way you thought it would—financially, spiritually, emotionally, relationally—or one or more of those categories feels out of sync with what you thought today would look like, fun is an integral part of what God has in store for you.

And the pursuit of fun will actually bring you some of the answers you hope exist, answers to some of the deep questions rooting around inside you.

A weird thing has happened to me since people started listening to the podcast. When people come up to me in public, whether it be at the airport or in a restaurant, at a coffee shop or at church, they often tell me what they do for fun.

Because we always talk about fun on the show. At the end of every episode, I ask each guest the exact same question: "What sounds fun to you?" And because listeners hear me ask that question twice a week, they want to answer it too.

It's hilarious, really, how much we want to talk about fun. I usually have to interrupt people and ask for their name because they are so quick to tell me their story that they forget to tell me what their parents put on their birth certificate the day they entered the world. So I stop the friend, ask their name, then tell them to continue. And once we've finished the conversation, their next question is "Can I tell you what I do for fun?"

And my answer is always yes.

Because I love fun.

WE FEEL SOMETHING lacking in our lives. We sense that this place in us that used to be filled just isn't anymore, even on our best days. It may just be a squeak sometimes, but other days it is a roar in our ears that something has been lost and we don't know how to find it and won't be able to find it. But we miss it. Because we know it used to be filled.

What is that thing? What are we missing that makes us feel its loss? You think I'm going to say fun here, and while that isn't wrong, I've realized that it's actually too simple an answer. But you know that, don't you?

You know that like I know that because it doesn't matter how hard we try or where we look, we can't seem to find that thing we've all lost. That buzz you get from a glass of wine won't get it back. His hand around your waist, while it feels awesome, doesn't return to you what you've lost. Even the best day lined up from start to finish still leaves you wondering if it's all going to crash down around you tomorrow. Because that thing, whatever it is, is still missing.

I saw a video on Instagram the other night (when I should have been sleeping) of an outdoor event where multiple massive games of Jenga were stacked on tables beside each other. You know the ones I am talking about? Where each Jenga piece, instead of being the size of a finger, is the size of a forearm. They were set all up and down two sides of a sidewalk in the middle of a grassy knoll. They were stacked and being carefully played by multiple groups of people. Everyone seemed to be having a great time playing these large versions of a fun group game. Suddenly, a college-age girl ran by the camera and shoved all five Jenga stacks, sending pieces flying. A drive-by (run-by?) destroying of everyone's good time. In the video, a woman screamed and people threw their hands in the air and everyone was super frustrated that they were playing a game until this girl came and crumbled everything.

After I watched that video, I couldn't fall asleep because I kept wondering if a cosmic version of that was going to happen in my life the next day.

I'm not here to tell you to carpe your diems. That's not the solution. To me that is just the other side of the same coin, asking where to find the thing we have lost and what's the quickest way to escape from here or fill in the gap of what is missing with anything we can find.

I think the truer statement is that what we have lost is real. That thing we know is missing is no joke. It's legit. While the world may look at your life and tell you that you have everything, you know the quiet, nagging whisper of truth. We have lost Eden, we have lost peace, we have lost the foundation upon which genuine fun can be built. And we have to go search for it.

So that's why we are here. That's the journey I've been on in my own life. A journey of sobriety (in more ways than you'd think), a rapelling trip into the depths of my own pain, a search for understanding. I thought I was writing a book about fun, but I realized we both need more than what that could offer. We need a way to find hope, to believe what we have lost can be found.

I think it can. But only if we will go where this story asks us to go. We cannot be afraid here—or at least, we cannot let the fear win. Let's all be brave, right? If we have to walk into our pain on the way to Eden, then so be it. Let's rebuild a foundation that used to exist just under our feet, so we can add layer upon layer of the good stuff, the heartbeats, the loud laughs, the tears of joy. Because, this won't surprise you, that sounds fun to me.

# Ebenezer Road

I WAS LUCKY ENOUGH to grow up on the same eighteen acres where my mother grew up. And for most of my life, my grandparents lived on the land as well. As you turn off Ebenezer Road—the double mailbox on your left, the gazebo covering a freshwater well on your right—the driveway crunches under your car tires because it is pure gravel. (Just ask my right elbow. I still have a pretty pronounced scar from a quick turn out of my grandparents' sidewalk on my bicycle sometime around third grade. I spilled. Hard. And my elbow can still prove it.)

The grapevines are there on your left as well, three rows of them, and if you look just over them, there's a small but impressive garden. The yard continues to the fence that touched our neighbor's property.

From Ebenezer Road, headed up the drive, my grandparents' house is on your right. And then on the left is our house, and just as you look past the front porch and the front door, you see a pond with a grassy trail circling full around it.

My grandfather moved to the farmland on Ebenezer Road in 1941. And for a time, it operated as such. By the time my parents were married and pregnant with me (the first grandchild), the place where the barn sat was better suited to be a home, so my parents built one. Within months after I was born, they moved out of my grandparents' house, where they had been living, just across the driveway to the house that would be ours.

I've ridden my bicycle over every inch of those eighteen acres. I've played house and played basketball and pretended to be a television host (me) interviewing guests (also me). I've built forts and created worlds and raced sticks down the creek behind the pond.

I have some of the weirdest memories of being little at that house. Running around in a summertime rainstorm in just my undies, while my mom sat on the porch, towel in hand. And like other young, murderous monsters (aka all of us), I caught fireflies and put them in jars with a few blades of grass and maybe poked two holes in the top of the metal lid. But my new pets were always dead the next morning. . . . Don't look at me like that, you KNOW you did it too.

I also remember snapping beans on the front porch of my grandparents' house while sitting next to my mom and my grandmother. My memory isn't precise, but in one particular recollection, some of the details are so strong. It was summer and I was wearing shorts, but it wasn't incredibly hot. Though to be honest, if we were snapping beans on the front porch on a summer evening in Georgia, it probably was hot. But my brain doesn't remember that part. There was one section of the porch that was always cool because it was always in the shade. The floor was cement and bordered with bricks. I can almost feel that spot again, my bare legs touching the cool cement, a colander in my lap.

The long beans were in a green plastic bag of some sort from the local farmers market, and we each had our own colander. The first move was to pull off the long string from the tip of the bean to the tail, then break the pod into three or four bean-length sections. You knew you'd gotten the right spot when it snapped. It's like the bean always knew. I was never a huge fan of chores, like many children I am sure, but there was something about snapping beans. It mattered. It was outside, it was with my family, it was a task that had a successful ending every time.

Snapping beans was simple. I wouldn't have been able to put that word around it as a child, but I know now that the spot it filled in me was the spot that loves simplicity. I don't know what was running through my grandmother's mind as she sat there, or my mother's, but I'm sure the task couldn't have felt as simple to them as it did to me. I was probably thinking about a book I was reading or a friend at school or absolutely nothing.

I miss thinking about nothing.

J. R. R. TOLKIEN ONCE WROTE, "Certainly there was an Eden on this very unhappy earth. We all long for it, and we are constantly glimpsing it."[1]

Eden is the first place humans ever lived, according to the Bible. In Genesis 2, before there was sin and before there was the brokenness we all feel, there was Eden. It was a garden and it was perfect. The humans there worked and gardened and cared for the animals and loved each other with no shame. And it was how things were always meant to be.

Though none of us have been there, don't you sometimes miss it? Maybe those simple memories of snapping beans are so strong because they feel like an Eden that I long for. My childhood was not perfect, but I do have certain memories, like snapping beans with my grandmother, that remind me of something that I feel has slipped through my fingers.

I SEE A NATUROPATH a few times a year. I started back in 2015 when I had this nagging cough and repeated laryngitis. I would speak at events on Friday and Saturday, lose my voice by Saturday night, whisper and cough until Monday or Tuesday, get a steroid shot on Thursday, and be back out on the road, preaching with my steroid-powered voice to a room of people, on Friday night. The pattern repeated for weeks, and each time I lost my voice, I was scared it might not come back. So a friend directed me to Robin, and through homeopathic remedies, oils, and supplements, we healed my body in a lot of different ways.

I saw Robin this week and told her some weird things that are going on with my body. I told her how it feels like everything inside of me is holding on and nothing is letting go. I feel big—not fat but solid, like I can't release things. We tested my emotions—the tightness between your emotional health and physical health is immense—and the main emotion that came up was a feeling of being abandoned.

That word appears almost every time she tests me.

But it doesn't make me cry. It doesn't bring up bad memories. I wasn't abandoned as a child, and I don't feel abandoned by a romantic partner. The actual definition of *abandon* is "lack of protection, support, or help from."[2] And as we read over the test results this time, I looked at Robin with clear and sober eyes and said, "Yes, that is true of me. I spend every day thinking about how I am in charge of myself, how no one else is thinking of me, how I have no covering."

It's a challenge for me to be single today. As my job and public image increase, my desire for a protector increases as well. And yes, I feel abandoned in the sense that I feel alone in my life. (I know married men and women who may feel the same thing—this isn't a uniquely unmarried feeling, but it is a feeling an unmarried person could have. Example, me.)

That feeling of being alone is not something I thought about when I was a kid on the cool cement porch snapping beans for dinner. I didn't think about a life at forty where I'm in charge of everything, a life where every buck stops with me. I wasn't thinking about bills or social media or growing a business or moving my laundry (IF THAT DRYER BEEPS ONE MORE TIME!) or what would happen to me at eighty-nine if I were still the only one in my family.

It was simpler then, with the beans on the porch. I was just Annie.


I THINK when we go looking for fun what we are actually looking for is home. We are looking for peace. We are looking for simplicity, something to fill that spot that has been left by growing up or growing out or moving on. While we think we want fun, what we really want is Eden.

A few years ago my parents moved to a new house. The one on Ebenezer Road wasn't the right fit for them after my grandparents passed away and all of us kids left home. I have struggled with my parents moving out of that house. To be fair, it's not my decision and I have no vote here. They deserve to live wherever they want to live. I moved my entire life to Nashville over a decade ago. They gave me that permission; I should offer them the same. But this loss has felt profound to me. All of our family events took place on those eighteen acres for our whole lives: Christmas mornings, Thanksgiving dinners, birthdays, random summer nights, Sunday after- noons after family lunch at a buffet restaurant down the street that made NEXT LEVEL delicious yeast rolls.

I asked my counselor about it a few weeks ago—why I want every man I date to see the old house, why I'm the one who got teary on Christmas, saying "I just want to go home," even though the whole family was together in my parents' beautiful new house. My counselor has a lot of thoughts. Most of them float around the idea of how safe I felt there and how many of my memories are tied to places, even more than people.

That's weird, right? Because I'm so extroverted you'd think I'd attach my memories to humans, but more often than not, my memories anchor in a place.

So while I know it isn't my house anymore, and while there are plenty of memories there that have shaped me in all the right ways and some of the wrong ways, I also know that I've lost something by losing the house on Ebenezer Road. I feel it deeply.

WE DON'T LIVE on a very good planet. (No offense, Earth.) It's just not going all that well here, is it? We have lost Eden in every way, but I've come to realize that it's the moments of fun that remind us that Eden ever existed in the first place. I may not be able to meet you there, but something inside of me knows what it feels like there. Something reminiscent of snapping beans on the front porch.

# The Movie Theater

I SAT ON MY FRIEND ELLIE'S PORCH last week, and right in the middle of the table was a bowl of green snap beans. Every now and again she would grab one and eat it raw. I sifted through my memory folders, and not once do I recall anyone in my family eating a raw snap bean as we were snapping. What a misstep on our part, apparently.

I blinked back to that memory of my childhood, that day when my little legs were crisscrossed on the cool cement, and I wondered why it had been so long since I felt that feeling. It zipped across my memory while I sat on Ellie's back porch, and my childhood was so close for a split second. There is something to those moments, something that is worth paying attention to and holding close. When we feel those moments, what are we meant to do with them or remember from them?

If you have eyes for providence, you will always see it. If you look for God's movement in your daily life, you will see Him. And I just keep finding that when moments like the one I had on Ellie's back porch lasso some long dropped-off memory, I need to pay attention.

One of the kindest things I've done for myself in the last decade is learn to pay attention to myself without judgment. When memories like that come to the front of my brain, I notice. They matter. They aren't something to be squashed or ignored. And as soon as that Ebenezer Road front porch memory ran through my mind and changed my heart and affected my stomach, I realized I felt the loss of it.

We may not have the words, or the exact knowledge of what those moments bring up, but we know something feels off. Even though we haven't been to Eden as it once was, even though we still have fun in our average day, even though most of us could say our day has gone well and the weekend is coming and we just found a great recipe to make on Sunday night, we feel the loss. And we think, *I just need more fun, I haven't done enough fun stuff lately.* So we start planning the next place we want to go. Or we don't, because we don't think of fun or plan for it or consider it something worth our time. We feel the loss and assume the feeling of emptiness it brings is a companion for life on Earth.

I HAD TO QUIT something I loved last year. I am still grieving it deeply, but the morning I made the final decision and the full day after, I was a weepy mess. Out of nowhere, my friend Heather texted me and asked if I had any free time the next day because she was available between ten and two while her daughters were in school. That next day was my Sabbath, my day off for the week, and I usually do not do any technology those days. But I needed to escape. I just had to get out of my life and my head. I checked the movie theater app, and the *Downton Abbey* movie was playing at 11:00 a.m.

I could not think of a more fun lunchtime hang than getting to escape with Heather and a box of Sno-Caps to the world of Downton Abbey, where the biggest problem is whether they'd be ready for a visit from the royals.

I put on a pair of yoga pants and a massive fleece even though it was still summer and was incredibly hot outside. But theaters are always cold, and I love going to the movies so much that I have to be comfortable. We sat in our assigned seats, and I turned my phone off. Not on silent—all the way off. I had to escape from all of it: the angry internet and the texts from friends. They were almost all supportive, so it wasn't that they were bad; they just made me sad. I needed to escape from all that my phone connected me to outside of Theater 24.

*Downton Abbey* was everything a thirtysomething girl with a predilection for British history could want. I cried a couple times but way less because of what was going on on-screen and way more because of the relief I felt falling into 1927 and the Downton world. It did not grieve me like my modern-day Wednesday grieved me.

SOMETIMES IN THE MIDDLE of a tragedy, someone needs to make you laugh. Sometimes in the middle of a heartbreak, you need to ride a roller coaster.

When he broke up with me on a Monday, I had tickets to see *Wicked* that coming Thursday with a bunch of friends. The woman playing Glinda the Good Witch was Ginna Claire Mason Moffett. She and I had connected on Twitter, and I had interviewed her for my podcast the week before. I loved her right away. Ginna Claire's parents live in Nashville, so we did the podcast interview on the floor of the guest room in her childhood home. It was a super funny way to record a conversation, but it made for the start of one of the dearest friendships in my life.

On Thursday, my girlfriends and I sat and enjoyed the show. I cried my way through two songs, wrapping myself up in the experience and also remembering that just outside those theater doors was a world where I was no longer in a relationship with that man. The show ended, and my group went to the stage door and waited for Ginna Claire's dad to come lead us backstage to her dressing room.

Ginna Claire had filled that dressing room to the brim with pink, including a step and repeat place: a long sheet hung by a curtain rod, where she could take pictures with friends and fans like us. You step in for a picture, step out, and repeat with the next person (hence the name "step and repeat"). Everyone met Ginna Claire and hugged her, and then we got to meet Mary Kate Morrissey, the incredibly talented woman who played Elphaba. Ginna Claire grabbed my hand and pulled me toward her dressing table and mirror, the kind with bright lights all the way around it. On the table beside her makeup and wigs sat a tiny tub of glitter. She opened it and carefully dipped her finger inside. Then she tapped her glittery finger to the side of my left eye and to the side of my right eye.

She didn't know about the man. She had no idea what was happening in my heart. But there was something in that moment that felt like a gift, felt like God reaching down and patting on my wounded heart.

Fun shows up like that sometimes. One of my favorite parts of hearing all my podcast guests talk about what sounds fun to them is the variety of answers I receive. People will tell of meals they have had that they'd like to have again, trips they are dreaming of, books they want to read, and people they want to spend time with. But every now and again, they just want to do something normal, self-labeled as "small." And even though those things aren't as flashy, fun shows up in those things too. It can be a vacation or a volunteer opportunity, friendship or fried foods. It's everywhere, if you're looking. If you let God gift you a glimpse of Eden, He will.

It matters that we talk about how to find fun in a life that doesn't always go the way we think it will. It is important for us to start finding the glitter on the days that hurt too much. (It doesn't have to be real glitter. I know most of y'all probably hate it.) We need to dream of foreign places and foreign languages and foreign foods on the tables where we sit and eat our everyday meals. Fun is a word we throw around a lot, me on a daily and pretty much constant basis, but it isn't as light and breezy as you think.

I saw a live podcast a few weeks ago, and the host, actor Dax Shepherd, gave the audience a couple minutes to ask questions. One young woman in the front row asked him, "How do you get through the hard times in life?" Dax didn't even pause. He looked her right in the eyes and said, "Just remember it always ends. You never get on a roller coaster and think, *This is so fun, I will be here forever.* The best things end, and so do the worst things. This will end."[1] I thought that was a profound and very tangible example for when we forget that the bad days don't last forever and that the good days don't last forever either.

But you know that. You know the rush always wears off. You know the laughter eventually stops. You know the sun will set, or rise, and the fun of today will end. It is one of the disappointing things about alcohol or a date or anything that seems to promise you a high that always lasts a few minutes less than you hoped it would. It ends. It always does. Even the purest, truest fun doesn't last forever. It is always a glimpse of something bigger, something we miss.

But that doesn't mean we stop asking the question, What sounds fun to you? In fact, I would say it is more necessary the more you understand that neither joy nor pain last forever, and it is far better to hold them both at the same time than to lean your life too heavily on one or the other. Knowing what sounds fun to you is about more than just filling your time and having an answer to a question at a party (or the end of a podcast interview). To know what sounds fun to you, what uniquely brings a level of joy and peace and simple rest to your heart, is what reminds you that God's journey for your life includes glimpses of Eden that show up in smile lines on your face and laughter that sounds just like you and art made from your unique spot on this planet.

Bonfire with friends LEANNE | Saturday mornings with my baby GINNER | World traveling with my sister MARY | Finding a new coffee shop CLARA | Curling up with a book EMILY | Laughing with my kiddos NIKI | Hanging out with my dog KATIE | A nice long run ALIDA | Cooking and eating with friends LIESEL | Slowly exploring a new city BETHANY | Mountains, coffee, marrying Mike MAGGIE | Having people at my table JULIE | Board game nights with food STEPHANIE | Vacation in Jamaica with hubs CLAIRE | Traveling with my adult kids LISA | Running my own nonprofit KARA | Going to the lake JENNA | A long weekend in Europe JENN | Coffee on the patio CHARITY | Riding a Jet-Ski SCOTTLYN | Doing anything with my family HEATHER | Beach trip with dear friends SARAH | Alabama football games CAMERON | Unknown child smiles at me LESLEY | Trolls movie-themed 39th birthday SARAH | Tacos and watching football HEATHER | Finishing my dissertation DEBRA | Going on an adventure KATIE | Eating sushi with my people TORI | Telestrations with our blended bunch ANNE | Trying new foods with hubby MÓNICA | Spending time with my people RILEY | Waterfall chasing around the world EMILY | Sunset on dock with friends DEBRA | Any "new-to-me" road LAURA | Road tripping with my girls KAYLA | Shelling on my favorite beach MISSY | Spending time with my people LUANN | Reading, music, coffee, chocolate, and nature TAMMY | Watching a Georgia football game KELLY | Cheering on the Braves MANDI | Hiking a trail LINDA | Christian concerts, friends, and family NATALIE | Always, another weekend in Paris ASHTON | Making a snow angel SARAH | Watching Hallmark movies and painting LIBBY | Coffee, conversation, and cool weather KATELYNN | Watching movies on a Saturday BETHANY | A day at the beach KAYLA | Cats in Christmas costumes MAGGIE | Finding new places to eat TODD | A beach in the Caribbean JANE | Family vacation EMILY | Going to Paris CHRISTIANA | Hanging with long-distance friends JESSICA | Running a marathon while juggling JILLIAN | Two weeks at Disney World SHANNON | Hiking with a friend AMANDA | Hiking with my family BARBARA | A long run with Macy ADRIENNE | Morning coffee with a country sunrise KELLIE | Sunny & 75, being outside STEPHANIE | Christmas music ALL YEAR LONG MINDY | Hammocks and a good book STEPHANIE | Traveling with my husband LISA | Laughing with my husband DEBRA | Travelling with my closest people COLLETTE | Sun. Fountain on. Backyard. Reading. LESLEY | Trying a new recipe STEPHANIE | Board games with nieces and nephews. CHRISTINE | Donuts. Latte. No calories. Guiltless. LESLEY | Traveling the world spreading Jesus NICO | Chasing sunsets JESSICA | Spending time with my children JENNIFER | Sitting at the beach with a book, enjoying the beauty of God all around me WILLETTA | Coffee shop hunting in Colombia MELANIE | See Wicked with Ginna Claire ELISABETH | High tea with my mom LESLEY | Walking my dog at sunset JESSICA | Ice-skating in Central Park MAGGIE | Hosting a quarterly Treasure Swap JOAN | Time with my people BETH | Saturday night between the hedges ALLISON | Hanging with the family cows ALEX | Gathering friends around my table EMILY | Taking a hip-hop dance class CHRISTINA | Making a life I love CAROLINE | Having coffee/conversations with friends JENNIFER | Build LEGO and drink beer BRETT | Beach with Cory, Grayson, and Camden WHITNEY | High tea with a friend RACHEL | Netflix binge with my friends LILLIAN | Traveling with my husband KAITLIN | Going to a Braves game ASHLEY | Creating and sharing authentic photographs EMILY | Adventures with my family AMY | Planning family travel adventures together MELANIE | Sister trip MADALYN | Breakfast date with my family KATIE | A TJ Maxx run with friends EMMA | Coffee with an old friend LEANNE | Being out of the rat race JENNIFER | Playing dress up with Dolly & Cher MIRANDA | Dancing around the kitchen cooking CHELSEA | Making new family memories MAGGIE | Gathering around the table CARMEN | A tiny, mobile house trip MICHELLE | Being a Golf Channel volunteer LAURA | Hawaii at sunset with family JULIE | Being in mountains with family EMILY | Hiking in the Tennessee hills MEREDITH | Greece with friends, eating baklava BROOKE | Going to Disneyland HANNAH | Time with my sisters MAYZIE | Lying on an empty beach HOLLIE | Broadway shows with my gals MEGAN | Going on a nature walk BETHANY | Adventures with Nathan, Uriah, and Bronx JESSICA | A weekend in Big Sur ERIKA | Road trips with my people KRISTI | Road trip with friends VICTORIA | Becoming an ASL interpreter BETHANY | Baking a homemade apple pie KAITLIN | Having a rad dance party LAINA | Outdoor activities with loved ones CHRISTA | Leggings and a jigsaw puzzle ANGELA | OKI, NC with my people JENNIFER | Unlimited play. Arcade to ourselves. LESLEY | Laughing with my husband LIZ | Hanging with LeeLee's Little Loves ALLISON | Being with my best friend KIM |

A kitchen full of friends MEG | Sunset dinner at the beach JESS | Traveling with friends and family MEREDITH | Hallmark movies in soft pajamas MADISON | Disney World with my family STEPHANIE | Chai tea with Annie and friends JENNIFER | Campfires under the stars SHERYN | Traveling and experiencing different cultures SARAH | A good book JENNIFER | BUYING A SPONTANEOUS PLANE TICKET ALLISON | Finding the best pizza everywhere STEPHANIE | Book, candle, quiet kinda day ABBIE | Running with my golden retriever HALEY | Food or coffee with friends WHITNEY | Any adventure with my family LESLIE | Outdoor adventures with my family MEGAN | Road tripping with my peeps KIM | Hiking with my little family LYNDSEY | Driving through the Arizona mountains CLAIRE | Coffee dates, baking & Christmas movies BETZY | Snuggling with my family EMMA | Walking on the beach ERICA | Vacay with JUST my husband JENNIFER | Road trip with my people NAKELI | Elton John kitchen dance party EMMA | Disney with my sister, Ruthie REBA | Being outside with my family DEANNA | Vacationing in Lofoten Islands, Norway NANCY | Golfing with my hubby WHITNEY | Sunday afternoon family game days LESLIE | Beach. Books. Husband. Sun. Rest. BECCA | Campfire sunsets with my people ERIN | Drinking coffee by Belvedere Castle MALLORY | Breakfast with my hubby LAURA | Laughing with my family BROOKE | Seeing Wicked on Broadway, again LEIGH | Eating Moe's with Sarah SAMANTHA | Reading by Christmas tree lights SARAH | A book at the beach JAMIE | Giggly adventures with my nephew SARAH | A walk, podcast, and coffee MARLA | Traveling the world, of course CHRISTINA | Long conversations with my husband SARAH | Hiking volcanos in Guatemala EMILY | Good coffee + good book + couch BEC | Michigan vacation with my mom MADISON | Hiking in the Colorado mountains ELIZABETH | Crafting with friends ALISSA | Reading books in a hammock SHANELLE | Coffee with a friend ABBIE | Paddleboarding with Jesus ASHLEY | Date with my husband HANNAH | Building a career I love HOPE | Getting a mani/pedi KEENAN | Family camp next summer MIKKI | Visiting all fifty states KRISTEN | Seeing God in the details LANIE | College football in the south ASHLEY | Dance party in the kitchen EVAN | Playing with all my grandbabies MICHELLE | Exploring, laughing, sharing with friends TARA | Surf fishing at Kure Beach BETH | My office's party planning committee BETH | Preparing a feast, Babette style SARAH | Being with my family outside MICHAEL | Date night + belly laughs ERIKA | Matching T-shirts in Disneyland HAILEE | Wandering on a mountain MADISON | Mountains. Chai. Worship music. Husband. ERIN | Snuggles, coffee, and podcasts ALICE | Relaxing at a resort pool BRIANNA | Grocery shopping & coffee talk PAULY | Bora Bora with my husband ANNE | Progressive dinner night out ROBYN | Cooking for special family meals CINDY | Melting glass on my torch LISA | Anything, anywhere with family SARAH | Travel with my family USA SONYA | Coffee with the Fab Five KELSEA | Singing with my Grammy SAM | Creating engaging themed classroom transformations JO | Painting my nails HEATHER | In nature with family MARYBETH | Spending time with my people NATALIE | Travel adventures with friends MARCIA | Quiet getaway in the mountains BRITTANY | Jumping on the trampoline EMILY | Watching the Dawgs win SEC SUSIE | Travel, bubble baths, kisses, beaches KIM | Watching college football win 2020 KARA | Concerts, concerts, concerts AMBER | Going to watch Braves baseball ELISABETH | Graduate PA school, pass PANCE MADISON | Having our firstborn in 2020 CHRISTINA | Reading by the fire ABBY | Playing in the Redcoat Band KATIE BETH | Having a family Christmas party LAUREN | Knitting by a cozy fireplace CARLI | Discovering coffeeshops in new cities ASHLEY | Vacationing in Israel with family LINDA | Cross-stitch and Hallmark GABY | Tacos, margaritas, girlfriends & laughter EMILY | Boondocking for free in camper CATHY | Exploring a new city AMY | Paddleboarding with friends DANIEL | Netflix binge with my friends LILLIAN | Great dinner with great conversation CASSANDRA | Reading by the Christmas tree ANALISE | Taking my son to the park KIERSTEN | Cookie decorating party MEREDITH | Watching Badger volleyball win JESSICA | Snuggling with my dog, Shirley ELENA | Off-roading tour in Moab, Utah SUSAN | Reading books by the fire MEAGAN | Creating art because God created ALEXA | Vacation with family in Scotland ESTHER | Boondocking our way to Texas SAM | Good scotch and great friends WILLY | Coffee with friends BAILEY | Experiencing joy, laugher, and happiness FAITH | Hiking with my dog, Bagel KATIE | Surprise weekend trip with hubby IVEYLEE | Family time with my teenagers MARCY | Laughing with my great love CASSE | Beach time with a book ELISABETH | Reading a good book KATIE | Hanging with my Young Life girls MAKENZIE | Time spent with my people LISA | Lay on hot sunny beach JULES | Discovering a new bird sound NANCY | Traveling the world MAEGAN |

Jumping into a ball pit LEIGH ANN | Friends, family, and live music AUTUMN | Walk, beach, husband, laughter, joy MARIE | Good book + cozy café JULIA | Hiking with friends in Colorado JULIA | My husband, coffee + Hallmark movies ELIZABETH | Anything Disney with my family NIFER | Girls' weekend with military spouses KENDRA | Beach day with my family JOANNA | Pack a suitcase and go DIANA | Coffee with besties ALLISON | Kids playgrounds at the beach VICTORIA | Learning to surf in Hawaii KAILEN | Hugging a cow EMILY | Swing dancing with my bestie KAILYN | Summer run with mind-expanding podcast DAVIS | Coffee with my sister LEANNE | Traveling with my husband AMY | Hiking through the Rocky Mountains CHARISSA | Date night with my husband DEEDEE | Going on a family walk ELLEN | The house all to myself ROBIN | Jeep ride with my hubby JAIME | Taking entire family to Maui KELSEY | Walking dog in autumn leaves JESS | Eating tacos with loved ones ELIZABETH | Adventures with people I love KATIE | Roller-skating and Krav Maga RACHEL | Beach, books, blue sky, shade PATRICIA | Laughing with my beautiful niece SHAUNA | Being in nature; feeling small COURTNEY | Charcuterie board with best friends HALEY | Vacation bike ride w/my family MARTHIE | Laughter-filled games with friends CHUI | Dinner with our whole family STEPHANIE | Paying off our house early SARAH | Meals with family and friends KATHERINE | Reading on the beach MALLORY | Reading on the beach DANIELLE | Girls trip with my sisters ABBY | Exploring coffee shops with friends HEATHER | SUP & sons' baseball games SARA | Going skydiving SHAWNA | Guacamole with family BAILEY | Walking outside, listening to podcasts LEIGH | Playing with my kids EMMA | Weekend away with friends JANET | Seeing a Broadway show BAILEY | Going to a livestock show TIFFANY | Eating with friends MELODY | Concerts with friends and family KAITLIN | Clearing land & burn piles JANELL | Puzzles with friends JENN | Visiting Graceland in Memphis, Tennessee ANGIE | Family+travel+running+cuddles+movies TARA | Leading my small group MERI | Cheering on the Georgia Bulldogs ABI | Coffee, wildflowers, sustainability, dancing, gathering JULIA | Hanging with family and friends MCKENZIE | Starbucks, Disney+, Christmas, friends, family BRITTANY | Road trip with my family KARISSA | Garden time, me and God ERIKA | Cuddling with my dog LAUREN | Playing with my dog, Mylo KYLE | Sharing life over coffee BRITTANY | Establishing an animal rescue MEREDITH | Morning coffee time with family KATRINA | Getting creative with God BRIANNA | Sacred laughter among kindred friends CHRISTY | Feet up. Eyes closed. *sigh* KARI | Young Life camp TAYLOR | Wedding then marriage this year AMANDA | Watching couples dance Latin Move YORCK | Cooking with my family LYNN | Walking in the woods LYNN | At home eating Abuela's tamales ELIZABETH | Christmas at the Plaza AMANDA | Afternoons of coffee & flowers DANIELLE | Disney with my little nieces RACHAEL | Traveling the world REGAN | Christmas lights, carols, family, eggnog KATI | My family Dancing and jumping through puddles RACHEL | A road trip with my sister ABI | Laura Cate and Hoke time JENNA | Making music with my husband MADDIE | My family living in Zambia KATY | Playing tennis LAURA | Playing music with my family ELLEN | A European river cruise MARY | North Shore, MN ANGELA | Hiking in mountains with friends BETHANY | Running marathons in new cities KIM | Hiking the Grand Canyon SABRINA | Sunrise bike ride MEGAN | Drinking coffee by the ocean ANGELA | Raising kids with my husband RUTH | Disney cruise to the Bahamas TAYLOR | 90s music dance party ANNIE | Beach day with my kids MEGAN | Slow Saturdays. Used bookstores. Coffee. CAMERON | Waiting for the sunrise LINDA | Going to Disney every week BETH | Family bonfire at NoBull Farm ELIZABETH | Making clothes for my kiddos OLIVIA | Beach time with my kids ELISA | Vacationing with family RACHEL | A walk in the woods MEGAN | Curling up with a book SYDNEY | With friends, laughing to tears NIKKI | Snuggling with my kids ELISA | Vacationing with family KARA | Cooking for family and friends ASHLEY | Being in the mountains JODI | Coffee shop and good conversations PAIGE | Gopher trapping LINDSAY | Partner adventure via VW van KALINA | Taking spontaneous trips with friends SHANICE | God laughing with me ERIN | Snuggling with my parents DOMINIC | Christmas caroling in July CASSANDRA | A vacation with my husband LAUREN | Riding a horse at sunset SHELBY | Going to Disneyland with family ASHLIE | Travel with family JULIE | Family beach trip for Thanksgiving AMI | Exploring, laughing, sharing with friends TARA | Road trips, skydiving, dinner with friends SYDNEY | Coffee with a sweet friend NATASHA | Gyming and listening to podcasts ZHONG YI | SUP in Fiji RUTH | Board games, laughing until crying KIRBY | The joy of supernatural peace JENN CARMEN | Secluded beach with my husband KRISTA | Taking a run-cation with friends CHRISTINE | Girls' weekend with my nieces CARI | Blanket forts with my nieces ROBYN | Prayer run at the lake ADENA | Laughing with my people KRISLYN |

Reading a good book SUZANNE | Surprise road trip with my bffs RILEY | Toes in sand JOHANNA | Taking entire family to Maui KELSEY | Road trips with my husband, Jordan COURTNEY | Food and games with friends LESLIE | Listening to someone's life story MARY | Hanging out with my family SUSAN | Time in the mountains REBECCA | Sleigh ride with my honey JULIA | Family dinner and game night SYBIL | Going to Disney World with family STEPHANIE | Going on a whimsical adventure EMMA | Puzzles with friends JENN | Quality time with my people MOLLY | Creating beautiful things with friends ANN | Concerts, food, and holidays REAGAN | Dancing and singing to musicals SARAH | Surprise birthday parties JESSICA | Christmas in Florida with family TATYANA | Any time spent with my people REBECCA | Grazing through Borough Market EMMELIE | Backpacking in Goat Rocks, Washington KAREN | Reading on a Hawaiian beach ALLISON | Being outside in the SNOW book HEIDI | My husband home from deployment KATIE | Virginia Tech football games KRISTEN | Opening nights at the theatre HEATHER | Spontaneous road trip with best friend CASSANDRA | Worshipping my King ELIZABETH | Exploring castles in Northern Ireland TAMMY | Going to sporting events CARLA | Sabbath dinner with my friends CORINNE | Catching a flight to Ireland SARA | Pressure washing. Yep. EVAN | Taking a long neighborhood walk KIM | Uninterrupted time with besties KATIE | Beach days with my husband JEN | Completing bucket list items TAMMY | Losing myself in music EVAN | Going for a walk ALYSSA | A competitive game of pickleball LINDSAY | Coffee + shopping spree MORGAN | Latch hooking by myself EMILY | Coffee in the mountains KELSEY | Getting lost in a book ALISSA | Taking curling lessons SARA | Hiking in the Smoky Mountains MADISON | Traveling with my dear friends CHRISTYANN | Being with my family TERESA | Camping in the Colorado mountains LINDY | Working to make dreams reality CARLY | A beach day with friends ALLISON | Family game night ALICIA | Eating the world's best cookie BECKY | Road tripping with friends KAYLA | Good hangs, food, and people SIERRA | Spending time with my sisters ANNE MARIE | Outdoor adventures with my kids MARIA | Long hikes with my dog AUDRYE | Driving around Ireland and Scotland SARAH | Go on a safari JERRAN | Getting my book published ANDREW | Wandering an art gallery alone KERI | Making croissants for friends MITTY | Stargazing JENNIFER | Beautiful food/drink with friends ASHLEY | First Christmas with my husband SARAH | Relaxing on the BEACH SARAH | Road trip with my besties JESSE | Slalom water skiing DIANE | Seasonal favorites: cardigans, candles, baking KARA | Camping, hiking, nature, sunsets, friends KAYLA | New socks, popcorn, watching movies SARA | Painting with my favorite people RYANN | A sweet getaway in Greece SARAH | Eating warm chocolate chip cookies VERONICA | Reading my Bible in Israel JORDAN | Trying new foods MAE ELIZABETH | Riding in an airboat JENNA | Singalongs with my sisters LEAH | Dancing to my phone strobe light MISSY | Game night with my favs ALLISON | Traveling to Africa w/ my nieces ELYSE | Playing with my dachshund puppies MADDIE | Doing absolutely NOTHING KAYLA | Getting lost in a book ALYSIA | Fishing JILLIAN | Italy in June JESSICA | Knitting in front of fire SUSAN | Dance party with my favs VALORIE | Going to the movies HANNAH | McKenzie River hammock hang time LORA | Hiking in mountains with hammock CHAD | Wearing matching shirts at Disneyland EVAN | Sidesplitting laughter SARAH | Dolphin watching and ocean swimming MIRANDA | Canoeing in wide, open waters JOYCE | Exploring a new city MINDY | Chicago pizza with friends GWEN | Mountain hikes and space walk JASON | Reading books about good stuff ROSIE | Tea and cake with friends JESSIE | A getaway with my husband SARAH | Singing in the ocean TIARNA | Road trip with my sister, Sarah KAIT K. | Singing Disney songs at karaoke JULIE | Sleep, coffee, family, friends, books LAUREN | Cooking dinner with my husband SARAH | Family. Friends. Reading. Hot tea. JESSE | Family movie day KATIE | Hawaii vacation with my family LYNNE | Beach trip with my kids JOIE | Disney vacation with my daughters SUSAN | Hiking in God's creation. ALEX | Eating my husband's cooking STEPHANIE | Travel, family, nature, quiet moments ASHLEY | Quality time with my daughters SUSAN | Cruise with my boys & husband BRITTANY | Be on TSF Podcast KAIT | Running at sunrise with B CARRIE | Going to Disneyland SARAH | Time with family, especially grandkids KAREN | All my siblings are home SARAH | Finding glory outdoors EMILY | Quality time with my kids DEBORAH | Game night with our friends MEGAN | To write someone's favorite song ASHTON | Being a woman in agriculture DARILYN | Putting together furniture JULIE | Hallmark Christmas movie marathon RAELYNN | Lazy day in the sun CARRIE | Time with my grown children LEA | Fireplace, tea, podcasts, laughter, tears KIM | Guilt-free naps every day SARAH | DANCING MERRILY | A long Sunday nap HANNA |

# The Joys
## of Being
## an Amateur

# The High Line Hotel

OFTEN WE USE the word *amateur* to describe someone who makes a mistake or handles something incorrectly. Like when I get on the wrong subway in New York City and start heading in the opposite direction of where I wanted to go, I roll my eyes at myself and think, *Amateur hour FOR SURE*. Because, honestly, what a dumb mistake to make. Or I'll bake a cake and it totally flops because I'm trying to make something dairy- and gluten-free, so it's not like a box of mix I can just dump into a bowl with an egg and some oil. It's a pile of unfamiliar ingredients from an incredible recipe created by Danielle Walker. But when the cake turns out more like a biscuit or a pudding—100 percent because of me, not because of the recipe—it's an amateur move. Because I don't know what I'm doing.

The actual definition of *amateur* is so much better than the meaning we give it.

Amateur (noun):
a person who engages in a study, sport, or other activity
    for pleasure rather than for financial benefit or profes-
    sional reasons

an athlete who has never competed for payment or for a
   monetary prize
a person inexperienced or unskilled in a particular activity
a person who admires something; devotee; fan[1]

Doing something for pleasure rather than for professional reasons. Admiring something and being devoted. It's like we've taken that ONE meaning of the word—someone who is unskilled—and made it the ONLY meaning of the word and slapped on a negative connotation. When we hear someone use that term, we automatically assume they have screwed up. We don't even consider that maybe they were just doing something for fun.

When did we stop doing things just for fun? I'm not talking about *we* as a culture; I'm talking about *we* as in you and me. When did we stop? And why? If our guts are always speaking to us about a way we are looking for Eden, then was there a point when we stopped doing things for fun and started requiring everything to be for profit or benefit? When did we decide being an amateur was such a bad thing?

Yes, that word means all the definitions you see above. It is an inexperienced person. For sure it is. But don't you just love the other definitions? The permission the others offer feels so good to me.

Dropping in to a new yoga class can feel so intimidating if you think everyone else is a regular and knows right where to put their mat or how many blocks of foam this teacher is going to want you to have. Going on a third date can feel incredibly scary if you think the person you are dating knows more than you do about where this thing is going. When pulling up to a church for the first time, it's hard to even know where to park your car. *Do I blink my emergency lights if I'm new here?* YEAH, ABSOLUTELY NOT! I'd rather park nine hundred miles away and walk barefoot to the door on a hot July day than park in the first spot and have all eyes on me as the "guest."

I hate being new at something because everyone is aware of my newness. Maybe you hate it too. Somewhere along the way we all decided we had to be professionals. That was the only option. It has totally stunted growth and squelched conversations and stopped us from being brave. If I think I can only do something I'm great at, or something I can fake greatness in, I will live a very limited life.

I think of this a lot when I think of Twitch streams, where professional video gamers teach the rest of us how to play certain games or get to certain levels. We watch the pros so when we play, we aren't amateurs. But we aren't playing at all, actually. We're just trying to get to the end with all the tricks we have learned from the pros who showed us all the moves. Or we watch eleven tutorials on creating the same eye makeup look and practice it multiple times at home alone before we'd ever just put on makeup and walk out the door.

Of course, learning and growing are important—and having teachers and mentors matters. But at the root of so many things, we don't want to look like we don't know what we are doing.

I worry about this a lot—the lack of joy associated with being an amateur. So many people in my direct circle of friends feel the pressure to be a professional. From new moms to first-time authors to singles moving to a new city, it's easy to think you have to do all the research and know all the things before you start. And then what? You should have done enough research about where to park or what food to feed the puppy or what neighborhood to move into that you don't make any mistakes. You're a pro.

But you're not. And neither am I. And it legitimately kills some degree of fun when we aren't allowed to be amateurs, by opportunity or by choice.

I've struggled hard with this concept, especially regarding social media. Thanks to the apps we all use, it is very difficult to live your daily life in public while learning and growing and making mistakes. A buzz phrase going around right now is "cancel culture." The idea is that when someone is found doing something wrong, their influence or popularity is immediately canceled. All the good they have done is erased and what is left is a bad taste in everyone's mouth.

There are times when the mistakes and sins are so massive and destructive and vast and habitual that the person should be removed from their position. But there are other times when it's just a tweet-sized mistake. But because we expect everyone to be pros, we have no space for anyone to be an amateur.

I understand this is a nuanced conversation to be having from where I am sitting and where you are sitting. But it is still true. How different would your life be tomorrow if you just gave everyone permission to not be professionals? It feels particularly close to me because I'm publicly navigating learning a few things I am not a pro at: how to be a female on a stage on a Sunday morning in a church, how to be a public-facing woman dating men who don't always want a public-facing relationship, and how to be a part of racial reconciliation and an ally for all sorts of people who are different from me. I want to be a professional at all of these things, but I'm not. What I am—what I can embrace—is holding all of these in the true spirit of an amateur who admires and enjoys and wants to engage in all of it.

So I'm learning. I'm trying to navigate dating well, with hopes of marriage and children in the future, but I've never dated with so much of my life public, instead of private. And there is no safety net. Whether he has a public life or not, I can't very easily hide when my heart is broken or when there are just a billion butterflies in my stomach because I'm so excited. There's a level of wisdom when I share what I share, but there's a difference in waiting to be wise and kind to my partner and waiting because I'm scared I'm going to do this wrong. I've tried it both ways, and they feel very, very different. (Also aren't you SO GLAD we don't use those labels on Facebook anymore like "It's complicated"? Gracious, I'm grateful we don't have to use labels on social media. DTRs, conversations where you Determine the Relationship, are hard enough without the added layer of "So what will our new status be on Facebook?" Yikes.)

Conversations where we are amateurs are still important to have. For example, let's talk about what it looks like to make sure friends of color feel welcomed in every space. Let's talk about how that has been done wrong and right in the past and talk about how each of us, no matter our color, wants to make it right, in and out of the church. But there is a problem. And that problem is fear. The voice of fear says it is better to say nothing at all than to speak up and risk saying something unprofessional or offensive. Just this week, one of my African American friends said to me, "I can't imagine what it is like to be learning all of this publicly—about the racial disunity and unlearning old ways of thinking." But what choice do I have? So much of my life is public that I can't imagine not sharing what I'm reading and learning. Does that mean I'm always doing it right or doing it well? Absolutely not. But gracious, what else can I do but try?

Actually, I know the answer. When you are an amateur, and a new opportunity comes along, you get to either try or not try. That's the other option. That's what else you can do. You can *not* try. You get to decide whether the thing in front of you is worth being new at, and maybe being an amateur at, in front of other people.

I wasn't an active part of the racial reconciliation conversation until I got a tweet from Kelli, an African American woman I didn't know. In her tweet, Kelli kindly asked if I would consider having more diverse voices on my podcast so that she could hear from some people who were more like her. I was here in New York City, right where I'm writing today, when the tweet came through and stopped me on the sidewalk.

Because she was right. I wasn't being thoughtful when it came to ensuring that my guest list reflects the varied faces of the kingdom of God. Not because I didn't want to or because I was purposefully being negligent, but I was passively negligent and unfortunately, passively racist. So I decided to change, and I started talking about it that day. In the next few weeks, I brought Kelli, the stranger-turned-friend, on my podcast and asked her to keep an eye out as I work to be more intentional moving forward. I privately and publicly apologized and repented. I began to follow a variety of voices on social media who don't look like me or think like me. I began to read pieces about racism and racial reconciliation. (I personally have found the work of Latasha Morrison and her book, *Be the Bridge*, incredibly helpful.) My team and I started being more thoughtful about the guests on the show, and we made a real point to give the microphone to people of different races who I was friends with or wanted to be friends with.

All of this is well and good, but I've made mistakes along the way, even just in my attempt to learn and share my learning. I am so late to this conversation and so new to talking about it publicly and sharing my opinions publicly that I feel it deeply when people are cruel to me online. I get super mad when people leave comments that question my motives or the reasons behind these new conversations. It is all hard. And it's all public. And I'm an amateur. I'm inexperienced and unskilled, but I'm trying. And, gracious, any conflict I feel from engaging in these conversations, for people of other races or the disabled or the underprivileged, is felt exponentially by those living those stories.

I'm not willing to be absent from the racial reconciliation conversation anymore—as a learner and listener first but also as a voice. It doesn't mean I know exactly how to handle every nuanced conversation that begins, but that is true in dating and in friendship and in work opportunities as well. Every day is the first day we've ever done today, so maybe there just needs to be a little more acknowledgment of the amateur who lives and actually thrives in each of us. I wonder if that's where the real return to Eden is, where the real world-changing stuff lives—in our amateur hearts.

THERE IS ANOTHER thing that can happen when you start something new—a relationship or a craft or a job or a conversation or a hobby. It's that thing where you try something new and you're actually great at it, like from very near to the start. You pick a handful of flowers from the yard and make a bouquet for the middle of the table before dinner and your guests are legitimately mesmerized by the beauty of what you made. You eat the most divine French onion soup at a restaurant and when you try to make it at home, adding the secret ingredient learned from Instagram (those ground up, dried mushrooms), it tastes exactly the same and the person you love across the table is blown away. You pick up an instrument and can play it. You watch one YouTube video on how to knit and by the end of a weekend, you've made a scarf.

Maybe your community is different from mine, but these days it just seems as soon as that happens, people quickly go from "Wow, that's good" to "Have you thought about selling that?" "You should arrange flowers for weddings." "You should sell that soup at the farmers market." "You should be in a band." You should, you should, you should.

People have lots of should ideas for those they think are professionals, or those they think SHOULD be professionals.

And when you listen to their advice and turn your fun into profit, suddenly you have a business, not a hobby. There's a demand that drives you to promote your product or idea, instead of just doing it—say it with me—for fun.

I'M CURRENTLY SITTING in the lobby of the High Line Hotel in New York City with one of my best friends, Jonathan Merritt. (He's an excellent author and a better man, and there is no one I prefer seeing obscure Broadway shows with than him.) It's almost 10:00 p.m., but my fingers are still moving across this keyboard, so I'm trusting them. People keep walking through the lobby, chatting with friends, heading to the bar, and meeting up with others. But the thing that keeps distracting me and making me laugh is the number of people who come through with their dogs.

One little pup, a French bulldog, is hanging out in the lobby with his leash dragging behind him. The valet, with whom the dog is clearly familiar, keeps messing with the bulldog. He is doing that thing that humans do to dogs: riling him up, messing with his legs and face, and rubbing his back and belly. The valet keeps making the dog growl then bark, and then the valet breaks into the biggest smile and looks around at all of us in the lobby to see who is laughing along with him.

His smile is so genuine, I almost can't look away.

As the bulldog follows the valet around the lobby, his leash dragging between those four short little legs, you can tell he wants more. And so does the valet. It's just so fun. There's something so pure about their friendship. The valet is currently standing over the dog, rubbing his back, and saying "good boy" over and over again.

(Also, I just learned the dog's name is George. Of course it is. That's perfect. Maybe he's a local hotel dog? Everyone who walks by, I'm hearing now, is speaking to George. Wait, is this dog famous?)

What I love about this interaction is that no one is making money off of it. It's just pure. It is a good reminder to me (and probably the valet, though I can't catch his attention to ask) of a time other than this. Other than here. No one is rushing up to the valet to say, "Dude, you are SO GOOD at petting that dog. Just look at how much you're smiling. Have you thought about changing jobs and becoming a dog petter?"

Right, of course they aren't. And this is a silly example, but it matters, because George is adorable but also because some things are just meant to be fun. Some things are meant to stay amateur level for us. Some things are meant to teach us and grow us and bring us joy, not income.

But there are other times when being an amateur is the first step in walking toward the thing that brings us joy AND income, brings God honor, changes lives, and feels like we're suddenly 100 percent right where we are supposed to be.

# *That Sounds Fun* Podcast Studio

I WAS LAUGHING so hard I was crying. While driving. Which isn't great. Except it WAS great. Sophie Hudson and Melanie Shankle were my first friends to have their own podcast—*The Big Boo Cast*. And it was just pure hilarity (still is).

In case the word *podcast* is foreign to you, I think it would be best described as an audio conversation or story that you can listen to on demand, through an app, on your phone, or via the internet. Imagine an old-time radio show when the whole family gathered around to listen, but instead of it airing Sunday nights at seven, once a podcast is released, it is available any time you want to listen. And it never goes away, so you can listen multiple times.

I lived in Kennesaw, Georgia, the first time I heard their podcast, and I remember hitting play on *The Big Boo Cast* as I turned out of my driveway on the way to work. I taught elementary school at the time so it was an early morning on the way to my classroom. I started laughing before I was even out of my neighborhood, and I was hardly breathing by the time I rolled through the stoplight.

Sophie and Melanie were telling a story about college football, if I remember correctly. That part has left my memory as it was probably twelve years ago or so, and it's definitely not the most important detail to remember about this story. Because what happened NEXT is incredibly memorable. I saw the light turn from yellow to red through tears of laughter, and I also saw the blue lights of a police car click on right behind me.

The weird part, or best part, about that day is that I couldn't stop laughing. I mean, I slowed down, of course, as I was getting pulled over. But I couldn't get my phone to stop the podcast, I couldn't find my insurance card fast enough, and I couldn't stop thinking of the story that Sophie and Melanie had been telling as I ran the light. So I just kept giggling—that church kind of giggling, where you KNOW you are supposed to stop but in no way do you know how to stop. And the added layer of weird is that it was 6:30 a.m. Anyone who is "church giggling" alone in their car at that time deserves to be pulled over. I respect that.

As the officer walked to my driver's side door, I was able to calm myself down and hand him the correct paperwork. When he asked why I ran the red light, I told the truth. I was listening to a podcast and was laughing too hard to pay attention.

I got a ticket.

(My friend Michael has told me a story of getting out of a ticket after being pulled over while listening to Drew Holcomb music because the cop also liked Drew Holcomb. Unfortunately for me, the particular policeman who pulled me over that day did not yet know and love *The Big Boo Cast*.)

But in spite of the fine I was charged, there was just something special about the conversation between two friends, playing through the speakers of my car, that felt like something I would love to be on the other side of too. I didn't know Melanie and Sophie very well at the time, but it sure felt like I did because of that podcast. I listened and felt like I could speak right back to them. They were friends of mine, whether they knew it or not.

YEARS LATER, the opportunity to start my own podcast showed up in my life in an incredibly unexpected way. Let me back up a little. You need to know that I am a huge fan of author Ted Dekker. His novels keep me up at night and make it impossible to do anything besides read at stoplights and while I'm drying my hair and pretty much any minute I can. After reading the first Ted Dekker books that came my way, I remember feeling like this author was equal parts brilliant and terrifying. That's a good writer.

In early 2014, my friend Jenn, who works for Ted, called me. I don't know how she knew that I loved Ted's writing, but she did. She told me he had a new novel coming out and asked if I wanted to interview him.

Of course, "interviewing" was not something I did on a regular basis back then. I didn't have a radio or television show. But a few years before that, someone had told me to always say yes. Even if you don't know how to do the thing someone is asking you to do (I didn't), even if you feel underqualified (I did), even if you are scared (I was)—if you want to try and the opportunity is in front of you, say yes, then figure it out. In sporty terms, you miss all the shots you never take.[1] I figured interviewing Ted was a shot I could miss and totally screw up, but I was at least going to try. So I said yes to Jenn. Of course I wanted to interview Ted Dekker.

At the time, I had a blog and a few social media accounts. I asked Jenn what she wanted me to do with the audio. She shrugged. I asked her how she was planning to release it. She said I should release it. I told her I didn't really have a platform for that, and she said, "Well, have you ever thought about starting a podcast?" And hand to heaven, I responded, "That sounds fun."

So the podcast was born to an amateur. It felt like the perfect name because that question—have you ever thought about starting a podcast—and the answer that came out of me, have been very directive in my life. The opportunity for fun, and the idea for fun, is always going to get a good and easy yes from me. It's the kryptonite and the invitation. Fun is what gets me up early and what keeps me up late.

I went home that day, googled "that sounds fun," and when I saw that no one had jumped on that title for a podcast, I did. Because, like I said, it just sounded fun to me.

I had no idea where this thing was going to go, but I wanted to make some early decisions, even if this was just going to last a few months. I made a few rules for my new podcast.

1. All the episodes would be thirty minutes long. (This has absolutely NOT remained one of the strong tenets of the show. My apologies.)
2. I would release one episode a month. (This has not remained the rule either, but I do not apologize for that.)

Jenn set up the interview with Ted Dekker in a tiny recording booth in a nondescript Nashville building where 21st Avenue meets Belmont Avenue. I made a list of questions I wanted to ask him, carefully numbered in order. (By the way, that is the most prep I've ever done for a podcast to this day—all has gone downhill since then.) Ted and I wouldn't be talking face-to-face, as he'd be calling in from his home in Texas and I'd be in the building on Belmont. I was given an early copy of his most recent novel and had absolutely devoured it. The downside is that it just increased my feeling of super-fandom toward him, which embarrassed me a bit and made me worry that I would never ever be able to be cool and professional in the interview.

It went fine. Ted was a very generous and thoughtful interviewee, and I didn't embarrass my friends and family with my fan-ness. The next day, the recording engineer sent me the raw file of the hour-long conversation, though I had no idea what to do with it. I turned to Google and started asking questions about how to edit and what programs to use and how to make a show out of this file. Because I wanted to have thirty-minute shows, I chopped Ted's interview into two parts and released them two Mondays in a row. I shared it on my blog and social media platforms, and a few hundred people downloaded and listened and seemed to really enjoy the recording. So I planned to do a few more. I called musician Dave Barnes, my friend and fellow author Emily P. Freeman, and one of my best friends Connor Harrell, who was playing professional baseball at the time. I bought a microphone off Amazon that was recommended by a friend, and I read an article on the internet about the best podcast-recording supplies. Suddenly I was set to create a podcast that would be released regularly.

IN THOSE FIRST TEN EPISODES or so of the show, I was doing every part of every episode—scheduling the interview, doing the interview, editing the interview, putting the show together (intros, interview, outro, and the music going up and down, which I am TERRIBLE at), uploading the show, sharing it, and doing the show notes. All of it. But I loved every second, even if I was terrible at some of the parts. It was just so fun. I loved the conversations the most. I worked hard at the rest of the show because I wanted to get to keep talking to people and sharing those chats. An amateur for sure, not making any money, not sure it was going to work, but having the world's very best time.

I never dreamed that being a big talker and an annoying question asker would ever turn into anything like this. It was just something that lived in me that I absolutely loved— talking to my friends, whom I find endlessly entertaining, and asking all the questions I've always wanted to ask. With a microphone there is added permission to keep asking. I knew I was an amateur. I hadn't taken any podcasting classes or interviewing courses. I didn't know how to use GarageBand well (or at all, actually). But what I knew, as the shows continued releasing to the world and as I kept falling more and more in love with this media medium, was that I wanted to keep going. I was fine being an amateur, doing something I loved for the pure joy of doing it.

Now we are years in and hundreds of episodes have been recorded and shared. You may have picked up this book because of a podcast episode that mattered to you, that connected us in ways you know. I often feel that connection too. You may be one of the very reasons I keep making episodes. (If you've listened to even one show then, yes, you are one of the reasons.) But I wonder if there is something in your life that you love enough to try it and share it with us? You don't have to be a professional, and it doesn't have to make you any money, but when you embrace the amateur in you, the things you love can start bubbling up and flowing out to the rest of us.

If you and I are already friends in any way (and even if we had no relationship before this book, I hope you feel like we're friends by now), here's one thing I know about you. You want to make a difference on this planet. You want to feel like you have FOUND THE THING and are DOING THE THING and that YOUR LIFE MATTERS.

One of my best friends called me the other day and said, "I don't know why I'm on Earth." It wasn't a suicidal statement; it was just her realization that she'd been on this planet for thirtyish years and had jobs and loves and homes and pets, but she wasn't sure why her life mattered. Why God made her in the first place.

We've all felt that, because, again, if we go back to Eden, we remember that part of what we were always supposed to do here is cultivate, grow, create, and tend. And there are days when we look at our lives and while we may have gone to work, done a good job, eaten a healthyish lunch, worked out, and then met friends for dinner, when we get home and crawl into bed, did any of it change the world? The day is gone, but did it matter? Do we matter?

Part of what we lost when we lost Eden was the simple understanding that our lives have purpose. The serpent still whispers, like he did in Eden, asking if we are SURE of what we know. Are we sure of what God said? Are we sure His promises are true? Are we sure that life has any kind of meaning beyond sunrise and sunset? (Spoiler alert: it totally does.) So listening to that urge inside your guts that says, "THIS is the thing that makes me feel most alive" matters, whether it stays amateur in your life or goes pro.

SOMETIMES STAYING AMATEUR is the exact right thing to do. I'm not saying you can't go pro with the thing you are loving as an amateur. (In fact, I have in some things.) But asking "Am I supposed to be a pro or am I supposed to be an amateur?" is the wrong question. The right question is "What brings flourishing in my life and the lives of the people I love?"

That's the goal here. To find what makes your heart flourish. It will feel like hard work and smell like long days and sometimes make you cry or throw your phone or swear you are going to quit at night, just to remind yourself in the morning that you didn't really mean it. But if your heart flourishes, if the enemy is silenced from telling you that your life doesn't matter, you know that even the tiniest steps toward something your guts are saying you are made to do are worth it.

Amateur or not.

# Disneyland

THE LAST MINUTES together really matter.

My previous assistant, Eliza, and I worked together for almost four years. She traveled thousands of miles with me and heard me tell the same jokes hundreds of times. She sat by me on planes; she sat far away from me on planes. I napped; she worked out. I wrote books; she napped. We ate at local restaurants and rented cars and earned Delta SkyMiles. We worked together, even while living in different cities, every day. Weekends meant travel to conferences and events.

And then one summer we knew it was time for her to get a new job and for me to get a new employee. Nothing went wrong; the calendar just turned over to a new season and we could both feel it. She's generous and kind and wanted to move on well, so she kept working for me through the end of the year. That gave us time to write up a full job description of what she had been doing and what I was going to want in her replacement. It gave us time to get everything set up and scheduled and to finish out our last tour season together.

Our final run of events was no joke. Four cities in two weeks: Los Angeles, Chicago, Orlando, New York. The trip started off with me speaking at a women's luncheon in California. We landed the night before, got the merch table all set up, and grabbed a quick dinner. We had a short meeting with the host of the event, who gave us a tour around the venue and a little bit of information—namely that she was a cast member at Disneyland. I can't tell you too much, but I can share that our host knew Cinderella. Like, she was beautiful and blonde and there was a time in her life when she REALLY knew Cinderella. (Ya with me?) This woman casually asked Eliza and me if we were interested in going to Disneyland.

I had never been to Disneyland and had only been to Disney World a few times in my whole life. But in an insane turn of events, just two months before this trip to Disneyland in California, I had the chance to go to Disney World with the creative team from my church. I'm not sure there is a place that makes me feel the way the Disney theme parks make me feel. I feel young and light and certain there is wonder and surprise around every corner. I smile the moment I step into the park, while I'm waiting in every line, and as soon as I get on and get off every ride. Of all the places I've been in my life, those parks are in the top tier of places that bring me the deepest joy. Again, it goes back to the childhood and Eden thing for me. The simpler my life was when I fell in love with those places, the further back the memories go and the more healing and dear the experience.

Eliza and I both knew that Disneyland was a good idea for us after the event was over. It was a luncheon, so by 3:00 p.m., we were cleaned up and packed up and changed into play clothes to head to the park. We were gifted beautiful rose gold Minnie Mouse ears, and I wore them with pride. It was the day of the SEC Championship football game and Georgia was playing, so I wore my long-sleeve, black Georgia T-shirt and jeans with my rose gold ears.

We bought our tickets and entered the park to see a massive crowd gathering right on Main Street U.S.A. It was a little before dinnertime, and apparently on one special Saturday near Christmastime, there is a candlelight event that "features a full Orchestra, Christmas Tree Chorus performing renditions of traditional Christmas songs and a retelling of the Christmas Story by a celebrity narrator."[1] On this particular night, a famous actor was reading, so the crowd was thick and excited. Eliza and I saw this as our opportunity to scoot past all the hubbub and the Christmas program and ride the rides with shorter lines, so we started buzzing our way through the park.

Fantasyland was our first stop. Walking through Sleeping Beauty's castle as the sun began to set actually felt magical. That may sound silly to you, but the temperature outside was that perfect California-December feel. It was cool enough to make me glad to be in long sleeves, but I wasn't cold. I was in comfortable shoes and had the ears on and was surrounded by happy kids and happy grown-ups and characters passing by. And there is just a feeling about Disneyland, especially for those of us who grew up watching Disney movies or knowing any of the history. You can feel the many years of that place in a profound and beautiful way.

Eliza wanted to ride the Mad Tea Party, so we did. I had never seen the spinning teacups in real life, only on the Disney Channel. They are special, it's true. The teacups spin under a canopy of leaves, and a few jewel-toned paper lanterns hang from the trees. There are ten different shades of pastel, and the faster you spin the steering wheel, the quicker your teacup goes around and around. The lanterns begin to fuzz together as you spin, and it's a beautiful scene.

I wanted to ride Peter Pan's Flight. On the other hand, I did not want to talk to Peter Pan the character, even though he was hanging around the entrance to the ride, because he was being VERY Peter Pan-ish. You know what I mean? I just wasn't in the mood for him to play a trick on me or mess up a selfie or do anything to ruin my very happy evening at Disneyland.

I have a clear childhood memory of riding the Peter Pan ride in Orlando. I remembered the hot-air balloons and flying over London. I knew it would feel sentimental for all the reasons I love the movie but also for the memories of riding it, but I didn't know it would make me cry. But alas, I was the thirtysomething woman crying her way around London and Neverland in sparkly Minnie Mouse ears. But to be honest, I was on the edge of puddling tears the entire night. Because even as we ran from ride to ride and grabbed dinner and churros and tried to sneak into Club 33, I always knew what this night was about. It was about an ending. It was a beautiful wrapping to an incredibly sad gift because this would be Eliza's and my last big adventure together.

We are adventure girls. And quasi-spontaneous trips like this one are my favorite. Eliza is the same way. It was one of the best parts of working and traveling together. Lobster in Maine. Pancakes in Pennsylvania. Sand dunes in Michigan. Icy waterfalls in Alaska. Soccer matches in Haiti. We never missed a chance to do something unique in the cities we visited. And this would be the last trip. Our Disney adventure the pinnacle memory. It doesn't get more fun and more memorable than seven hours in Disneyland in December.

Our bodies were on our home time zones, so we both felt a little wonky as the night ended, but we had done it all. Leaving was sad because we were tired and the park was closing, but leaving was also sad because we couldn't pretend it wasn't a bigger ending than just that day.

I didn't know how to hold both of those things: the joy of Disneyland and the grief of a life we'd grown accustomed to ending. But I knew we had to do it. I knew we needed the memory, even if we didn't know how to imagine a life where we didn't work together and see each other every day on FaceTime or every weekend on an airplane.

We have to walk each other through grief, even when we don't know how to do it. Actually, we don't have to. We get to. We get to ride Peter Pan twice just so the memory sticks like glue. We get to walk down Main Street U.S.A. as it (fake) snows on our heads and the smell of gingerbread fills the night air. We get to be amateurs, doing things we don't know how to do but doing them together. There's a purity in that, in this, and in walking through something we don't understand to get to somewhere we've never been, and really genuinely feeling it all the way.

I know that about both Eliza and me. We weren't escaping; we weren't using the evening in Disneyland to not feel the sadness of no longer working together. Disneyland was a gift within the pain, and in a way, the fun was part of the grieving. We drank deep of it, and as the book of Psalms says, even in laughter our hearts ached.

# Dollywood

I WENT TO DOLLYWOOD for the first time for my musician friend Hillary's birthday about ten years ago. Being at Dollywood with a country music star really works in your VIP favor, and we had the absolute best time. But I hadn't been back again until this spring. I was speaking in Pigeon Forge when a friend from the Dollywood PR team, Amber, invited Emma, my tour manager for the weekend, and me to come to the park.

From the first minute we walked through the gate, we were smiling and having fun. We rode roller coasters and toured Dolly's Tennessee Mountain Home and the chapel—both exact replicas of the real things. We spent a surprising amount of time looking at the bald eagles in the bird sanctuary and we ate cinnamon bread. I didn't know this before that trip, but the cinnamon bread is legendary. Before it's baked, the loaves get absolutely drenched in butter and then smothered in cinnamon sugar. And when they bake, they bake all the way through but are still somehow incredibly gooey. Emma and I split some and were in awe and heaven and every other word you can use to describe that kind of delicious.

It felt sweet, in a more than just a cinnamon sugar kind of way, to be there with Emma. In a new season where Eliza was no longer my travel buddy and coworker, and when my new assistant, Jenna, wasn't available to go, Emma was the perfect companion. Emma is a touring professional, so I knew I could trust her with the work side of what we were doing. But she's also a very close friend who knows me really well and loves, loves, loves to have fun. In fact, she rode roller coasters I wouldn't ride because I didn't want to scramble my brains and risk getting a migraine.

It was a really fun day.

I GOT AN EMAIL from Amber early in the fall, a few months after that trip with Emma, that there would be a Hallmark Christmas movie filmed at Dollywood, and in the email she asked if my friends and I would be interested in being extras.

My amateur heart answered yes, yes, a thousand times, yes.

If there is a Venn diagram of the Hallmark Channel and Dollywood, I promise you I am the center where the two circles meet.

My friends Jami and Jennifer came with me to Dollywood because they are the official Hallmark Christmas movie experts in my life. They watch many of them, they love most of them, they dislike a few of them, and they can talk about all of them. Every year we record an episode of the *That Sounds Fun* podcast about Hallmark Christmas movies. We talk about the best ones to watch, our favorite actors and actresses, the ones that make us roll our eyes, and the scenery that seems real and the scenery that seems fake. (Canadian mountains look nothing like the Smoky Mountains. Just a thought, Hallmark. Love you, mean it.) So when this opportunity to be an extra came to me through the same friend from the PR team at Dollywood, and I knew Jami and Jennifer would be on the podcast soon for our yearly episode, I asked and Amber said it was fine for them to come with. Jenna came too because how dare I have an absolutely fun and excellent experience without her?

We arrived at Dollywood at 10:00 a.m., having left Nashville at 5:30 a.m. The night before we left, I was stressed and tired and didn't read the email sent to us by Hallmark, so I did not realize I wasn't wearing the right-colored shirt until we had already filled out our paperwork to be extras and were walking into the park.

It's hard to know what to expect when you've never been an extra in a movie before. It's that amateur life again, isn't it? I had such high expectations for this day—I knew I wanted to tell you about it here, I knew it involved Dolly Parton, Dollywood, Hallmark, my friends. It felt like this day, this story, was going to be the pot of gold at the end of the rainbow that started way back with the migraines and the bed rest and the whole fall season off the road.

The park was beautifully decorated for Christmas. Lights were strung up everywhere in every color, Christmas trees lined the sidewalks, and garland and decor hung from the light poles. It was extraordinary. A few members of the film crew walked us to Red's, the fifties-themed restaurant in the center of the park. It was around 11:00 a.m., and there was a large group of friends and family members of Dollywood employees together in there, including us, who would be extras for this movie. We picked a table, got our computers out, and all four of us got to work on some things we needed to get done. We knew there would be lots of waiting around, so we had all brought things to do.

We got to shoot one scene early in the day. It was an outside shot where a five-piece bluegrass band played in a small gazebo. We were standing in front swaying. You'll see us doing some great acting. I'm the girl with brown hair in the winter coat. ☺

After that scene was done, we went back to Red's around 12:30 p.m., and sat back down. It started to rain. Every now and again for the next few hours, a member of the crew would come into the restaurant and pull a few extras to be in scenes. But they never chose us.

Dinner was served, and we were getting antsy. We knew the shoot was supposed to go until 11:00 p.m., but the rain had changed so many of the shoot locations from outside to inside that they needed significantly fewer extras than originally planned. The four of us were still having fun, laughing together, telling stories, working, and snacking. We even went outside at one point when the rain stopped and took a picture for me to send as my Christmas card.

After the sun had set, a member of the crew came and collected about one hundred of the extras, leaving only about twenty of us in the restaurant. We didn't know what to do. Should we just keep waiting? Were we missing the biggest scenes and maybe missing our chance to see Dolly Parton herself?

I had such high expectations for what the day would look like and what it could be. And here we were, leftovers in the holding pen, rain pouring outside, the clock ticking. I felt the pressure as the contact person between my friends and PR Amber.

I work really hard to be patient, to wait, to not rush things. I'm naturally not patient, so when moments like this present themselves, I feel so torn. OF COURSE I wanted to be out there, but were we supposed to let our patience muscles grow in strength? My insides were in knots, not knowing the right thing to do. Text Amber and tell her where we were or just keep waiting?

My friends made the call for me. I texted Amber.

I told her we didn't even care about being in the movie, we just wanted to be on set and stand with her and see it being filmed. Amber walked to Red's in less than five minutes and took us with her to set, apologizing like crazy for not realizing we weren't in the big group of extras standing in front of the main Dollywood sign, where a stage had been erected for a concert scene with that same bluegrass band we had seen play hours before.

As we walked up, I turned and looked at the sign, and just through the opening in the *D* of the massive Dollywood letters, I saw sequins. Lots of them. All of them. And blonde hair. And there, just thirty feet in front of me, was Dolly Parton. I couldn't believe it, and tears came to my eyes before I even realized it. We broke every rule and jumped into the scene, walking back and forth in front of the stage where she and the other Hallmark actors were dialoging back and forth. We ate a moon pie from catering (food that was meant for the famous people in the movie, not leftover extras like us), and we stood under the entrance portico and let the heaters warm us up while we watched the scenes in front of us. We weren't in the movie anymore, but this view and experience was even better. We saw Dolly so clearly and so up close. I watched as the director coached and taught a young cameraman how to get the shots they needed. I got to see them build the sliding track for the moving camera and then just as quickly disassemble it and rebuild it in a new location. I saw Dolly's nephew, who is almost famous himself, as her longtime bodyguard. It was an absolute fun feast for my eyes and my ears. None of the extras were allowed to have their phones or cameras but because we were with Amber, we were considered media, so we have tons documented from that day: pictures from up close with the Hallmark stars, selfies with Dolly in the back, shots of the set. What a gift!

They were planning to film for two days, but we could only stay for the first day. But the four of us just kept saying to each other, and to Amber, that the experience was better than we could have dreamed. Amber was sorry we weren't seeing Glacier Ridge, the higher part of the park that was already decorated for Christmas in blues and whites and ready for filming on the second day. We had seen Main Street decorated, but we would be missing Glacier Ridge.

A little before midnight, just before the last scene of the night wrapped up, we walked back to Red's with Amber and packed up our things. We were ahead of the rest of the extras returning from set, so the restaurant was empty. We laughed at how many hours we had spent in that place, memorialized our table, and got our things together. Just as we were headed out the door, a young midtwenties girl, who was working on the movie as a production assistant, walked in and asked if anyone else needed a ride to parking lot G. Our car was in that lot, so she said she would drive us over if we all loaded up on her golf cart.

As we started on the drive, the production assistant driver gal mentioned that one little road was shut down by construction so we'd have to take what she labeled "the long way" to the parking lot.

The park was empty as we drove, but all the Christmas lights in the different areas were twinkling. It was cold and windy but beautiful. And then suddenly, we turned a corner, and Amber had a knowing side smile on her face as we crested into what looked like thousands of blue and white lights. Glacier Ridge. The long way to the parking lot took us straight through the area we wouldn't get to see the next night. It was silent and empty except for us.

And we were silent, too, because the view was just breathtaking, and being the only people in the moment was something special.

If we had gotten picked to be extras when we wanted to get picked . . .

If I hadn't texted Amber . . .

If we had left early because we weren't sure we'd be in a scene at all . . .

If we had walked back to Red's ten minutes earlier like I had wanted to . . .

We would have missed Glacier Ridge.

And we would have missed seeing it together.

We didn't take any pictures together up there. We were smooshed on a golf cart and bundled up to stay warm, but I don't think I'll ever forget it.


THE DAY DID NOT UNFOLD as I predicted. It wasn't Eden as I imagined it in my mind. It wasn't the pot of gold at the end of a rainbow, but maybe I don't want the pot of gold. Maybe what we've actually always wanted is the rainbow. That's the only thing we can see anyway. There never has been a pot of gold. But there have always been rainbows.

That day, my friend David texted and asked how everything was going, right around when the pizza arrived for dinner, our third meal at the same table in Dollywood. I told him about the rain and the sitting and the waiting, but I also told him we were telling stories and laughing and he said, "Most anything CAN be fun. It just depends on us."

And I said, "Yes. I want to get THAT as a tattoo."

Most anything can be fun. It just depends on us.

Not just me and not just you. It depends on us. I think that may be the secret sauce here. Eden wasn't complete with just Adam. Before the snake, before sin, before anything went wrong, it was already wrong for Adam to be alone.

The joys of being an amateur are better when we aren't alone in them.

Life is just better *with* than *without*.

FUN CAN SNEAK UP on you like that. You think it's going to be starring in a Hallmark Christmas movie, and it's actually a golf cart ride over Glacier Ridge. It's why I love asking my podcast guests what they like to do for fun. I love hearing the variety of answers, the many ways people have fun, and how often it involves other people, a twist in the story, or a memory worth making.

I will never forget that day at Dollywood. That park is quickly becoming one of my very favorite places. But even more than seeing Dolly Parton up close and seeing the behind-the-scenes details of a big-deal movie being filmed, I will never forget being with my friends and watching God unfold for us a day we couldn't have dreamed up ourselves.

Oh, and by the way, since the park was closed, we couldn't get any cinnamon bread. So the next morning as we headed back to Nashville, we swung by the DreamMore Resort—the only other place that has the cinnamon bread—and bought two loaves. It was absolutely delicious.

# The Dock

Heading to Athens, Georgia, for college was the first time I ever moved in my life. Now trust me, since then I've had enough addresses that it makes background checks complicated to list them all. But before college, my family had always lived on Ebenezer Road. I didn't know any other home.

When my parents purchased their new property and planned to move, they called us all and planned one final family meal together at the house on Ebenezer Road. Their home, and my grandparents' house across the driveway (with the cement porch perfect for snapping beans), was where every family meal and holiday had been celebrated for the last forty years at least. I have cousins who live all over the country and even in other countries, so when the ones who live in Asia were planning a summer trip home, we knew it was a good time to gather.

It was Edenish in the most heartbreaking ways. What I wanted most was to be at my grandparents' house, for my grandfather to be grilling chicken and ribs, for the sound of the window units to fill the air, and for the grown-ups to be at one table and all the kids to be at another. I wanted to barely be worried about what was happening anywhere beyond those eighteen acres. I wanted to have a book tucked under my leg at the dinner table, probably a Garfield comic book, just hoping for a chance to sneak away and read. I wanted my grandmother to be laughing in the chair at the end of the grown-up table in the dining room, legs and arms crossed, her pants and her top the same color.

And we were so close. SO CLOSE to that. My parents and uncle were there and in great health, but my grandparents were gone, and their house wasn't ours to use anymore. Dad was incredibly good at grilling and his burgers were unmatched, but the outside grill where my grandfather cooked the meat, a rectangle of cement and stone, was broken down and full of leaves and debris and hadn't been used in decades. The kids at the kids table were now the adults at the second table. We were all grown, and there were so many worries outside the property that there was no magic way to leave them sitting at the end of the driveway. I felt a certain depth to this meal, knowing it would be our last with everyone on Ebenezer Road.

We did that thing where we all stood on the porch for a picture in the same spots we had always stood so that we could mark growth and change over the decades of taking the same cousin picture. We caught up and laughed and spent the afternoon helping Mom and Dad with the food, cleaning up the kitchen afterward, watching a baseball game on television, and talking. We were always talking. As the sun set and the blue darkness of a July summer sky took over, it was my time to shine.

I had made a decision on the way down from Nashville, my Toyota RAV4 driving that well-worn path between Music City and Atlanta—I-24 East to I-75 South. I would not stop anyone (myself included) from feeling sadness or pain about the loss of this house and this property, and I would do my part to make the whole thing fun. To me, making strong fun memories are some of the best ways to partner with the pain you feel and give it purpose. Fun is never meant to replace pain, or better said, fun will never replace pain. But fun can walk alongside it. You can hold them both and see what happens when they dance together.

My mom used to say that I was a thermostat for our family and it made me feel massive pressure, like I would never live up to controlling all the emotions in everyone. If I was in a bad mood, I just wanted to be in a bad mood and not have it affect everyone else. But that's not real life for the way God made me. It took me until my late twenties to find the joy and purpose in that role in the family, but once I got more emotionally healthy as Annie, I got more emotionally healthy in my role in our family system. (I am a lot of other things in our family, too, but I do recognize the spot I have is the gift of helping us see things in a different way; therefore, I often bring a new perspective and an added helping of joy.)

So about an hour into my three-and-a-half-hour drive, I pulled off the interstate before reaching Chattanooga. There was a massive warehouse just off the exit with huge red letters painted on the side that spelled FIREWORKS. I had never been in that warehouse before, but I knew that drive was the perfect time to stop.

I walked in and pretty much just said, "Give me one of each." Just kidding. I'm not rich and my RAV4 doesn't have that much trunk space. But I did buy far more fireworks than we needed. I got a few packs that made me laugh—a bunch that were named after presidents of the United States, some random ones that just looked fun and colorful, and then a bunch of the long tubes that you hold while multiple fireworks burst out of the end. (I think they are called Roman candles.) I got ten of those. One for each adult cousin and cousin spouse in our family, and then one extra just for fun. I also got sparklers because those seem like the exact right thing to have on hand at all times. (So says the girl who keeps a drawer full of confetti poppers at her office AND her house.) Once the back of my car was filled absolutely to the brim with entertaining explosives, I got back on the road and continued my drive.

After dinner that night on Ebenezer Road, when all was cleaned and the sun had set, all the grown-up kids headed down to the dock at the pond. The pond isn't large; it's maybe an acre total, and it was manmade back in the farm days of the land. The wooden dock has about a fifteen-foot walkway from the edge of the pond out to a platform. I'm not sure the exact measurements of it, but I can tell you it is nine adult cousins wide, because we all stood shoulder to shoulder to shoot off fireworks.

We started with the ones that we set down and lit the fuse and ran away from. As they exploded into the sky and reflected on the still water of the pond, they were beautiful and hilarious and no one was injured in the lighting of an entire savings account worth of fireworks. We had our own show, and it was glorious. Then the Roman candles were all that were left. We each lit one and stood in a straight line and let them explode over the water, watching them burst from each of our cardboard tubes. And while I didn't cry, I felt it deeply. I felt the joy of the moment and the absolute beauty of the experience, but I also felt the loss. There's a version of Annie that would have required me to pick one—either love it or lose it—but the more God has formed me and transformed me, the more I have room for both.

I'M NOT A PROFESSIONAL at grief. I'm not actually a professional at fun either, though I do feel like I've put enough practice and hours to get some sort of credit for what I know about it. Finding fun in the midst of grief is one of the things at which I always want to be an amateur.

Finding fun, making memories, bringing a smile to a situation that is full of sadness and pain—these are all things I want to engage in for pleasure and things I feel devoted to. I refuse to force grief to be a quick experience. Back in Bible times, it was customary to grieve for a week after someone died. Like when Lazarus died in John 11, Mary's friends were sitting around weeping with her for four days after her brother had passed. Then when she suddenly jumped up to go find Jesus on the road to Bethany, they all followed, still full of sadness, thinking she was going to her brother's tomb. They were still weeping after FOUR WHOLE DAYS.

We've shortened the grieving process these days, but real, true, deep grieving lasts much longer than the amount of time we're given to be sad. Nowadays you have less than a week to grieve before life moves on, the internet moves on, your friends move on. Of course you will be sad, but we'd like you to keep that to yourself and only your very best friends, please. We have moved on.

(I think we are doing that wrong, by the way. We should notice each other's grief and choose to acknowledge when others are suffering and slow down enough to let each other feel sad as long as we need to. But that's another book for another time.)

I'm no professional at grieving, but honestly none of us are. We are all amateurs at loving and losing, because each circumstance and situation is different. Every relationship that ends is different from the one before. Every friendship that falls apart pings unique spots of pain. When a person dies whom you have known and loved, the loss is unlike any other loss you've experienced.

In a way that people cannot see, there is a unique grief to losing dreams that will never be fulfilled or jobs that you weren't hired to do or homes that are no longer yours. There are losses that no one else sees, grieving that is so deeply private, that while the rest of your life could look right in space and place, you know profoundly that Eden is lost.

This is true for everyone. Every one of us. While we are all amateurs, we are not that different than our neighbor or friend or family member or archnemesis. We are all very new to grief and pain, every time, and we all know it.

But we also know the release of a laugh and the freedom of a smile in a heartbreaking moment. We know that there can be joy in grief. That's the magic trick here; that's the piece you have to search for and find and give to your people. Every time you provide a smile amid tears, every time you get cookies delivered to a teenager at the hospital just because you know she loves warm cookies, every time you think of that one little fun thing that may make someone else's day better, the people you are serving with your fun are getting a glimpse at Eden, and so are you.

I TEXTED MY COUSIN TODAY to ask him the name of that particular firework, the Roman candle, because all the ways I tried to google it based on what I remembered about how they work led me down some weird paths. My cousin lives in a part of Asia where the time difference is twelve hours from Nashville. I never calculate well, so I just kinda go for it and text him when he comes to mind and hope and pray I don't wake the poor kid up with some stupid meme I INSIST on sending at that exact moment. (I am the oldest in our family, so in some respects, I am allowed to be the most annoying. I embrace THAT role in our family system with much gusto.) I was surprised when he texted me the answer almost immediately, and then he asked, "Gathering fireworks for Thanksgiving this year?" I laughed. But it spoke something to me too.

It reminded me that my amateur move of buying a bunch of fireworks just to help us remember a special night for our family stuck with all of them too.

Understanding others through the Enneagram KIMBERLY | Moving in worship and praise HEIDI | Watching the Seahawks win ALYSSA | Grocery store with mom EMILY | Hiking His creation SARAH | Beach vacation with good books SARAH | Hiking in foggy mountain air RACHEL | Beautiful beach with my husband MICHELE | Chocolate, good book, quiet house ELIZABETH | Taking singing lessons REBECCA | Having my newborn in January MARIAH | Making pies with Nan CAIT | Coffee with a close friend SHAUNA | Traveling with my family CHRISTI | Baking pies for family/friends ANGELA | Hiking with my husband/puppy ZOE | Watching a beach sunset MAGGIE | Exploring local spots with friends DEA | Going for a bike ride MIRANDA | Anything with my husband ANGELA | Fly-fishing BANNER | Beach day with my people HANNAH | Hanging out with my sisters COURTNEY | Sleeping on the beach ABBIE | Road trips and coffee shops COLLEEN | Disneyland with my friends TERESA | Surfing a non-baby wave KENDAL | Skydiving—even if I'm scared TERA | Bath bomb in a HUGE tub ALICIA | Dance party with my friends KATEY | Hanging out with miniBFFs DANIELLE | Summertime outdoor country music concert ANNA | Finishing graduate school in May KACEY | Karaoke with my dad ASHLEY | Giggling with my littlest friends ESTHER | Movie night with my family ASHLEY | Cooking dinner with my husband MADELINE | Walking my big dog, Trig TIFFANY | Coffee shops in the mountains MADDIE | Friends' trip to Kenya DAWNA | Spending uninterrupted time with girlfriends JENNY | Weekend of laughter with girlfriends LISA | Being with my people JESS | Reading ALL the books MICHELE | Weekend getaway with my husband JANNA | Israel David Branch, adopted grandson CINDY | Beach reads along ocean waves KELLY | Good food with good friends ABBEY | Spending time in the mountains MARSHAN | Board games with my family KRISTEN | Beach time with loved ones AMY | Fripp Island with my family EMILY | Going to Hawaii with friends ROSE | Coffee and small-town shops KIM | Coaching volleyball BEKAH | A good farmers market KIM | Going on a hike LISA | Reading at the beach LAUREN | Launching TSJG, living big dreams SARAH | Good food with great friends KRISTIN | World trip with my family MEGHAN | Baking with my three-year-old son SARA | Coffee shops & my family SYDNEY | Getting to marry my fiancé COURTNEY | Sitting on a beach DIANA | The lake with my family MORGAN | Traveling with my husband CHARLOTTE | 30-A VACA with my people LAURA | Family cross-country road trip MICHELLE | Hammock nap in the sun KATIE | Crosswords with husband and Hallmark HEATHER | Going to Italy LILY | Morning run then family brunch LAUREN | Spending time on the water BREE | Days in my front yard LACEY | Visiting Canada with a friend MARIA | Marrying my best friend on 3/7/2020 MEGAN | Large table of friends eating KIM | Books & coffee shops by the beach MICHELLE | Spending time with my family TAMMY | Roaming Christmas markets in Germany ALLISON | Coast-to-coast road trip MELISSA | Reading a book with tea LAURA | Gathering around tables with friends TIFFANY | Traveling with my family KASEY | Date night with my husband SARAH | Barre and breakfast in Santa Barbara AMANDA | Cooking a phenomenal meal OLIVIA | Taking a trip to Utah MEGAN | Girlfriends, wine, and beach vacation LISA | Playing board games with family ERIN | Bike rides with friends JENNY | Adventures with my friends CATHY | Reading books on the beach BRANDY | Amusement parks with my family SARAH | Snuggling with my cat ELLIE | Holly. Karen. New York City. SAMANTHA | Long walks with my Pomeranians JESSIE | Paragliding through mountains in Scotland KAITLYN | Beach trips with family & friends BECCA | National parks road trip with friends EMILY | Game nights MIRANDA | Travel around Europe with friends HEATHER | Road tripping with my sisters BECKY | Reading on my back porch JESSICA | Bikes, hikes, bonfires, and friends JESS | Going somewhere I haven't been JENNIFER | Family time in national parks ANDY | Food and wine with friends LAURA | Relaxing beach trip KAYLA | Game night with my family BRIANNA | Girlfriends' weekend at the lake house KAREN | Having a bonfire with friends JOANN | Playing trucks with my toddler CARRIE | Dance party in my bedroom JESSICA | Coffee in a rocking chair MOLLIE | Reading cuddled under a blanket RACHEL | On the beach with my daughter MELISSA | Traveling with people I love PRISCILLA | Being at the beach MEAGAN | Jesus moments, daughters, belly laughs, coffee KRISTEN | Being one with nature MELISSA | Music around piano with family HEIDI | Snuggled up with Hallmark Channel AMBER | Walks with my dog REBECCA | Snuggled up watching Hallmark Movies TORI | Dogsledding on fresh-groomed trail JUDY | Playing with my chickens PATRICE | Fostering a houseful of boys SHANEN | Trust falls and high kicks BRITTNEY | Hanging with friends and #minibffs KATRINA | Coffee/hot chocolate with family TIFFANY | Game night with friends KATIE | Lying on the beach BROOKE |

Climbing mountains with friends CAROL | Family, good food around a table YANET | Country line dancing KELSEY | Spending time with my people SARAH | Disney with my favorite people HALEY | Hike with dogs and friends DANNI | Eating French fries and donuts RHONDA | Getting to travel with Hubs LINDSAY | The beach with my family HEATHER | Family, friends, serving God, Disney ASHLEY JEAN | Mountain biking with friends TJ | Retreat with fun/deep friendships ANNE | Cruise with my family NATALIE | Watching Hallmark movies all day CORINNE | Snuggling my three boys TARA | Doing life with my husband NATALIE | Morning. Porch. Coffee. Good book. AMY | Snuggling my MIRACLE newborn baby ABIGAIL | Hiking the Grand Canyon rim-to-rim JESS | Traveling. Seeing God's Work. FENWAY | Watching movies with my kids. CHRISTINE | Flourishing in my marriage SARA | Bargain shopping online STEPHANIE | Traveling to new places ALICIA | Cuddling with my furbabies JENNI | Beach vacation with my husband RACHEL | Hiking in the Jessamine Gorge KAITY | Eating with friends HAYLEY | Beach + books + bubble baths + music ROBYN | Reading fiction on the beach ELLEN | Crochet crafting with Hallmark movies CHRISTIANN | Friday night movie with family ANA | Coffee with my besties—always JESSIE | The beach with my people EMILY | Spontaneous road trips with friends BEKAH | Watching my kids play sports CATHERINE | Playing board games with my kids DESI | Puzzling. Hot Chocolate. Harry Potter. CASEY | Slow Saturday morning, good coffee KATIE | Walking with my baby girl LAUREN | Making others laugh JENN | North Georgia Mountains with friends SARAH | Road trips with girlfriends/sisters DEE | Dance party CALEY | Taking my daughters to the ocean EMILY | Big charcuterie dinner party SHEA | Going on a BFF girls' trip MAGGIE | Family game by a campfire HEIDI | Building a cheese/charcuterie board ANNA | Uninterrupted time with God VAL | Playing with my dog MADYSEN | Going to Bear Paw JENNIFER | Vacations with my family CHRISTI | West Wing with my hubby CARLA | Date night with my wife PHILIPPE | Loving others and bringing joy AMY | Tourist-ing in my city HALEY | Hiking in God's beautiful creation KRISTIN | Conversations around a fire pit MICHELLE | Going on mission trips MELISSA | Hanging with my family DEMETRIA | Freedom in Christ to be myself KENDA | Traveling somewhere with good friends ALYSSA | Perfect Day at Coco Cay MISSY | Drinking some warm coffee REAGAN | Confetti cupcakes with pink frosting LAURA | Beach vaca with the fam MADELINE | Disney World with my family LINDSEY | Bubble bath & a good book JENNIFER | Christmas with my sweet hubby DORI | Confetti cannons, friends, and cookies ERIN | Coffee, family hike, ice cream, nap CHELSEA | Trying a new cookie recipe EMILY | Communing with my best pals RILEY | Reading a book on beach RACHEL | Teaching phonics KENZIE | A quiet cabin with friends CHELSEA | Squishing Jell-O with my feet JOANNE | Swimming in Lake Michigan TRACEY | Spending TIME with my family KATEY | Scalp massage at the salon JOANNE | Going kayaking with friends STACEY | Watching Broadway shows with friends CHELSEA | Reading fiction novels with tea ALLISON | GIRLS' TRIP LIZ | Hiking trip with my friends NICOLE | Porch sitting with my husband KELLY | Listening to podcasts while baking LIZZIE | Visiting Nashville someday soon ERIN | Shopping spree of ethical brands MICHELLE | Visiting my BFF in Vegas TINA | Decorating my new house EVE | Bonfire with my people EZRI | A trip to Paris CHRIS | Walking my dog somewhere beautiful KATIE | Family friends singing, dancing, reading KATIE | Road trip across the US JESSICA | Going south for the winter PATRICIA | Leading worship at my church RACHEL | Visit old Peace Corps community COURTNEY | Beach + crab + raspberry sparkling water TARA | Walking with dogs & hubby ABBY | Opening a coffee shop in 2020 KELSEY | Going on a surprise trip DANIELLE | FOOD, shows, silliness w/ loved ones OLIVIA | Catching frogs in a sundress CHRISTINA | Drinking hot tea and reading AUTUMN | Playing golf with my family SARAH | Breakfast with my husband KACEY | Sewing (particularly for gifts) #sentimental KEELY | Any excuse to use glitter MOLLIE | Friends, laughing, music, tea, sunshine EMILY | Traveling somewhere sunny for tacos AMANDA | Being in Disneyland with Dad KELSEY | Having coffee with my daughter KIM | Sitting by a Colorado waterfall JILL | Spending quality time TAYLOR | A campfire with my people KELLEY | Showing sheep with family SARAH | Good food, friends, and puppies TARA | Sunrise beach walk with dogs EDEN | Thanking Christy Nockels in person MEREDITH | Games with family and friends CHELSI | Aimlessly exploring a new city ANNA | Family. Friends. Outside. Together. LAUREN | Exploring in God's beautiful creation BRITTNEY | Honeymooning in Hawaii KEELY | Running a marathon LAURA | High school youth group ministry LEIGHA |

my chair MEAGAN | Watching the sunset at sea LESLIE | Family beach trip ANDI | Traveling Europe with my husband with friends JORDAN | Any adventure with my people ASHLEY | Orangetheory with all my friends SAMUEL | Performing Wandering through the Botanical Gardens HOLLY | Watching Hallmark movies with friends GRACE | Good wanderlust SARA | Ice cream dates with family CAROLYN | Books & friends by the water ANNA | Reading on the beach with my family JENN | The beach with my family COURTNEY | Drinking the world's best coffee ABBEY | Watching SHANNON | Experiencing any new culture SARAH | Road trip with my girlfriends ANGIE | Wine nights with Lauren B MEGAN | husband ABBEY | Hiking followed by a bonfire KRISTEN | Traveling the world with Brian EMILY | Moments with my husband/kids

Coffee, pjs, books, and MELISSA | Trip to NYC in a musical JUDITH | coffee & fueling my KRISTIN | Traveling Sweet Sadie ice skate Spontaneous trip with my DAWN | The simple things in life JOANNE | Coffee at the lake JILLIAN | Trip to London with family AIMEE | Walking by the water MARIA | Living a life set apart BISCUIT | Baking cookies with my family JULIA | Petting all the dogs HANNAH | One-woman car musicals MICHALA | Cabin with fire and snow ALLISON | Go to a movie matinee LORI | Suntanning and gelato in Tofino BECKY & DAVE | Running in the REVEL Marathon DAVE | Sharing adventures with my people ANA | Going to the Outer Banks GINGER | Sunshine, hubby, and Segway adventures JENNIE | Podcast listening while walking dogs MICHELLE | Walking my two dogs ALISON | Photographing food BECCA | Massive road trip across US MADISON | Sunshine & the beach BETH | Diet Coke & Pinterest SHANNON | Anything outside JARED | Mini Coopers, confetti, sprinkles & friends IRIS | Going to Disney World ELLIE | Wandering beautiful food markets EMILY | Babymoon with my hubby ROSIE | Napping in a hammock ABBY | Hiking, margaritas, friends LAUREN | Going hiking with my husband CARA | Europe adventure with the #cacklepack EMMA | Time with my best friends AMY | Sharing the Gospel with everyone KRYSTAL | Anything to do with wine CAITY | Family, friends, kids, travel, hiking DEBBI | DISNEY ALL DAY CHRISTI | Exploring new places with family TYLER | Yardsaling with friends in summer LISA | Marriage, SARAH | Family walks RACHEL | Hiking a mountain with friends JULIA | Drinking Chemex coffee with friends CAREN | Playing with baby elephants SHANNON | Spa day and a nap JENNIFER | babies, ALL the charcuterie JENNIFER | Thrifting BECCA | Beach trip with college besties CAREN | Going to a Braves game RYANN | Disney World anniversary LINDSEY | Girls' weekend away with BFF LAURA | Disneyland with 100 friends LAUREL | Spending time with loved ones NICHOLE | Doing life with my people TALOR | Hiking at Radnor Lake MAKAILA | Beach Disney World vacations ANNA | Spending time with my family CLAUDIA | Wandering the library TIFFANY | Hike with my family AMY | Going to Disney World EMILY | Reading a book on beach PAULA | Vacations (anywhere) with my family AMY | Outdoor weekend with no phone LACEY | People watching at the airport ERICA | Going to tea with friends BETHANY | Traveling and exploring new places SADIE | Cross-country road trip LEE | Seeing my family again AMBER | Laughter, popcorn, and Beyoncé Knowles COLLEEN | Hiking with my sweet husky KAYLA | Traveling to Europe BLAIR | Beach, book, Diet Coke KATIE | Escaping to the movies LOUISE | Watching God connect His people MARCI | Exploring coastal towns with family KIM | Plant shopping with my bestie ALEXANDRIA | Pick-up soccer ABBEY | Hiking in the Colorado mountains KAREN | Growing my sweet little family KRISTIN | Cross-country motorcycle trip JEREMY | Running through Charlotte in prayer KARLEIGH | Beach. Beer. Ocean with Wife. JEREMY | Wine night with girlfriends. LITHA | Long run in the sun LEAH | Parenting girls toward trusting Jesus LESLEE | Horseback riding JAYLA | Hot coffee, friends, and quilting SHANNON | Beach getaway with my husband MARISSA | Travel to Israel for the first time MARY | Cat cuddles and Hallmark movies JENNA | Learning. Podcasts. Friends. Family. Fitness. SALLY | Traveling and exploring the world BRITTNEY | Going to the beach with family ROBYN | Being on an airplane JILL | Hosting wine night with friends LINLEY | Hot apple cider while reading MADELYN | Deep talks with my BFFs SABRINA | Playing outside with my family AUBREY | Anything with my niece, Audrey ANNIE | Paddleboarding with my people KATIE | Going to a NKOTB concert LESLEY | Beach, friends, dancing & pizza LAURA | Running while listening to TSF pod GRACE | Exploring London with my husband ASHLEY | Water-skiing a peaceful mountain lake MELISSA | Traveling Israel with my Dad MEG | Cartwheels with my kids BRIANA | Family biking in Hilton Head KELLEY | Christmas lights and peppermint mocha JORDAN | Traveling new places with friends ANNIE | Belly-laughing with friends JILL | Reading uninterrupted at the beach JILL |

World Cup with my people JENN | Complete aloneness with my husband AMANDA | Dinner and games with friends GINNY | Hallmark movies with Diet Coke CARRIE | Reading in a coffee shop SARAH | Adventuring with baby girl Atlas SARA | Spontaneous road trips to the beach TAWNI | Teaching yoga at the beach KATIE | Baking and trying new recipes BETHANY | Every second with Gabe Willison PAULA | Talking Enneagram with a friend ADRIA | Video games with my kids MOLLY | Day at the lake LAURA | Winery + spa + girlfriends MELISSA | Making homemade ice cream ELISE | Snuggling up with a good book EMILY | Holy Yoga in the garage JULIE | Snowy day, coffee, and books RACHEL | Skydiving TASHANA | Quality time with my people KERI | Finally graduating from nursing school BRYNNAN | Brisk walk with my puppy ELIZABETH | Laughing with my family ASHLEY | Being by the ocean STEPHANIE BYERS | Take my husband to Disneyland NAOMI | Beach with my family ALLANA | Swinging and looking at the sky AMANDA | A wedding dance party KIM | Kayaking with beluga whales AMBER | Writing letters in a hammock EMILY | Traveling with my family PJ | Warm, sun, beaches, friends, family JENNIFER | Toes in the sand TRACY | Disney World with my daughter JEN | Family. Sunsets. Coffee. Snowflakes. Music. JENNY | Travel, dogs, family, and friends. JAYME | Laughing with friends by fire EMILY | Being on my paddleboard MELISSA | Raising a strong, BRAVE daughter ANNA | Adventuring with my lifelong friends ALLIA | Relaxing in a candlelit bath KRYSTIN | Family, friends, food, movies, sleep JENNIFER | Running a marathon KAT | Board games with loved ones DORA | Skiing the mountains with family ASHLYN | Taking a bubble bath EMILY | Gospel conversations around African food VANESSA | Walking around a new city HANNA | Bodysurfing in Carlsbad ILISE | Date night with my husband BRANDY | Hammocking by the lake MCGEE | Walks with my dog, Maggie KATE | Taking my son on adventures XOCHIL | Weekend away with adult children FONDA | A beach day with friends MAEGAN | Beach trip with the family KERRY | S'mores around the campfire ELISABETH | Friday night homemade pizza night MELISSA | Someday, HEAVEN. What an adventure! REBEKAH | A day at the beach AMY | Visiting my niece and nephew MARNIE | Saturday coffee with my mom AUDRA | Unexpected interruptions to love well KELLIRAE | Vacation with my people LAUREN | A room full of kittens LOUISE | Starting a new book DOREEN | Fall weather and porch time KATE | Riding horses on the beach BRIE | Hanging with my dogs/husband ALEXIS | Family hike at the lake ASHLEY | Drinking and brewing espresso MANDI | Skydiving with friends MALLORIE | Girls' trip with my friends JORDAN | Mystery novels on rainy days KIM | A walk outside in fall LESLIE | Rainy Sunday with worship music MARLENE | Hiking mountain trails with pals CINDY | Hanging out with my girlfriends MICHELLE | Family, friends, food, and concerts AMANDA | Dancing in the woods EMMA | Chicago summer days HANNAH | Wearing glitter with Ginna Claire ALLISON | Time with my hubby, Carter MARISA | Being cozy in a quiet room LAURA | Painting Disney World CARTER | Good book on the beach HEATHER | Being in nature with family STACIE | Iced coffee on Main Street U.S.A. SUZI | Taking a hike KELLI | Coffee and conversation with friends ANNA | Connecting heart to heart BETHANY | Long baths with books RACHEL | Cooking for my friends MONICA | Dinner with friends ABBY | Dressing up and going dancing KAYLA | Watching movies with my fiancé ALBERTO | Grocery store with Mom EMILY | Loving life with my family MARLA | Puppy snuggles and good wine HOLLY | Rainy day coffee shop writing KATHLEEN | Endless time with my besties MICHELLE | Going to Jeremy Camp concerts JACKIE | Knitting all day long BRITTANY | A book that evokes feeling MICHELLE | Hiking South Sister in Oregon MACKENZIE | Quilting with friends LISA | Watching Hallmark's Signed, Sealed, Delivered KAYCEE | Hammock, Spikeball, sunset, bonfire, fireworks JORDAN | Hanging out at the beach GEM | Day with my family JAMIE | New city adventures with family SHANNON | Hanging out with my husband MADELYN | Laughing with friends in nature TRICIA | Traveling the world with friends ALLISON | Sitting on a mountain JOANNA | Lying on the beach BROOKE | A for KING & COUNTRY concert DAYSHA | Yummy dinner with my friends ANDREA | Braves season tickets #chopon AMANDA | A hammock in the sun RACHEL | Reading a book in sunshine ANNIE | Being GOOFY KRISTEN | BIRTHDAYS—mine and others MELISSA | Day on lake with family MANDY | Spending time with my girlfriends to Orchestra and Zumba with my family KRISTIN | Coffee shops with friends JESSIE | European vacation with husband BETHANY | Going SARAH | Confetti poppers in EMMA | Planning a party for friends AMANDA | Beaching with dog and husband LIZ | Acting in a Disney musical Family. Music. Bonfire. my purse JULIANA | Weekend getaway with best friends RACHEL | DANCE PARTY with my people KRISTINA | and friends beach day SHAN | Food. Laughter. AMY | Coffee and a great book ELIZABETH | Family vacation to Hawaii BETHANY | Family

Snuggling up with my dogs MEGAN | Coffee dates with Christ ALIE | Being on the lake AMANDA | Going to a live musical NIKKI | Chocolate, friends, and laughter MEGAN | Family, friends, food, fitness & faith ANGI | Making up silly songs HAYLEY | Bath, wine, and a book GRACE | Mountain cabin girls' trip JEN | Disney with family and friends ANGI | Learning, laughing, leading, loving CHRISTOPHER | Book, blanket, fireplace, and nap AARON | Impromptu sushi dinners with friends STEPH | Crafting & Christmas movies BETHANY | Reuniting with my Ohio tribe CAROLYN | Hike in every national park CHRISTY | East Africa on mission trip TRACY | Family, food, stories, and laughter JILL | Wine and cheese with friends ANNE | All G-kids in one place G-MA | Trout fishing ERIN | Milkshakes on Balboa Beach, CA CASSANDRA | Road trip adventure—no responsibilities JESSICA | Books. Tea. Outside. Music. Hammock. JULIANN | Football Saturdays with my husband MALLORY | Soaking in a mountain sunrise KYLIE | Tableside guac with friends JENNIFER | Playing with Wiley, my dog STEPH | Disco night with disco lights KAYLA | Reading at the beach DEBORAH | Building houses with Amor ministry MICHELLE | Book. Warm drink. Cozy throw. KARIN | Rollerblading with my husband LAUREN | Vacation with my friends HEATHER | Unlimited chips and salsa buffet JOY | Quilting with friends LISA | Sharing stories & laughs while adventuring KAY | Coffee, my kids, laughing together BECKY | Visiting Italy with my husband ALLISON | Pawhuska, Oklahoma, with my sister JEN | Watching Hallmark with my cat ELISE | Riding bikes with friends BESS | Coffee with my coffee BFF COLLEEN | Family vacation in Mexico TINA | FIVE DAUGHTERS BAKERY ROBIN | A day of music and sun MEGHAN | Drinking coffee by a mountain COLLEEN | Adventuring with my family JESSI | Friends, food, fire, surfing & wasabi SKYE | Skydiving with friends KIRSTEN | Frozen pizza and movie dates TANNER | Beach with family BARBARA | Exploring every US National Park KELLY | A horse and a sunset TERA | Mountains with family and friends JANE | Campfires late with my husband BETHANY | Playing on swings SAMANTHA | All-inclusive tropical resort with family HANNAH | Spending Christmas with my family LYDIA | Having four sons LINDSEY | Mocha at beach and with good friends ERIN | Coffee and traveling with friends KIM | Seeing Mumford live eight times NATASHA | Dallas Mavs game with family KIMBERLY | Adventures with family and friends BETSY | Road tripping with my hubby ALISHA | Exploring new places with friends JORI | Running a marathon KEATYN | Live music JESSICA | Getting married in February <3 KRISTLE | Seeing Mumford ten times :) BRIGITTE | Visiting Glacier National Park SYDNEY | Traveling the world with family HELEN | Vacation at the beach KELLY | Tea and conversation with friends RACHEL | Coffee with Grant in Vancouver HANNAH | Baking new desserts & breads RACHEL | Coffee with a friend SUE | New passport stamps + good friends KIM | Schlitterbahn in New Braunfels, Texas KELSEY | Football Saturdays in the South COREY | Speaking words drenched in beauty KIERSTIE | Dancing like no one's watching KRISTA | Serving Jesus and my church KAYLA | Sunday night family dinner LAUREN | RVing and hiking BRENDA | Watching Olympic athletes win medals AMANDA | Worshiping around a campfire MADDY | Going to a great concert ALLI | A solitary voyage to someplace new CLARA | Hiking on a sunny day MADDIE | Going to Lesotho or Zimbabwe MORGAN | Laughing with my family KARLYN | Hiking the Pacific Northwest CECILY | One long nap, then Disneyland ALLYSSA | Snowboarding in the Alps KRISTEN | Surprising people with gifts KELLY | Seeing the zoo's red pandas AMANDA | Music, video games, good food DAVID | Walking on an Australian beach LEANNE | Late-night chats with friends MICHAELLA | A road trip with friends MELISSA | Adventuring in Australia BRIGETTA | Lochs. Swimming. Firepit. Friends. Whisky CIARA | Beach dancing with friends HELEN | Running barefoot through mud puddles CASSANDRA | Firepits, friends, baking, camping, live music NICKY | Ice cream and Hallmark movies BROOKE | Lying on a beach ERIN | Snowshoeing in the Rocky Mountains JENNA | Going on a coffee tour JOY | Jumping in leaves with kids KERI | London with my people ERIKA | Baking with my family HANNA | Going to France REBECCA | Marrying my long-distance honey CAITLIN | Going back to Kenya MICHAELA | Looking at my old yearbooks KERI | Launching my own creative business RACHEL | Holding my baby in July SABRINA | Disney+ all day in PJs ELIZABETH | Piano lessons at age fifty-three LESLEY | Target and Starbucks NATALIE | Bowling WHITNEY | Coffee and a good book BEKAH | Mani, pedi, and massage KIM | Disney World and unlimited FastPasses NISHA | ANYTHING NEW TO ME MELISSA | Making s'mores over a fire ABBY | Visiting our friends in Germany CORI | Time with those I love MARIA | The BEACH. ALWAYS. CATHERINE | Playing games with my people RACHAEL | Learning a new creative skill. NAOMI |

# The Power
## of Falling
### in Love

# Haggart's 1801

I FALL IN LOVE CONSTANTLY. All the time. I fall in love with ideas and I fall in love with the laughter of children. I fall in love with movies and I fall in love with recipes. I fall in love with the waiter who describes a wine perfectly and I fall in love with the handsome single man who volunteers at church. I fall in love with meals and I fall in love with jackets from shops in Aberfeldy, Scotland.

Haggart's 1801, a little shop in Aberfeldy, Scotland, wasn't even open when we walked by in the late afternoon on an August day. But I looked in the window and absolutely loved everything. There were three of us. My American friend Laura, my Scottish friend Ciara, and me. Ciara knew the shop owner, Ryan Hannigan, was inside so she opened the door and invited us in. Ryan was kind and let us look through what he was making, and in less than one second, I fell in love with a jacket. His custom tweed lined the inside of a grey vintage Swiss army jacket. The buttons were perfect, and soon I was begging him to sell me a jacket on a day his shop wasn't even open. But I was in love. (I still am. I love that jacket so much.)

And I'm not being insensitive or crass with the word *love* like they used to tell us in church—that people use *love* too liberally and don't really know what it means . . . blah blah blah. I absolutely mean this. I feel love big. I feel everything very big. I don't feel one thing small. I feel big happy and big sad. I feel big excitement and big yikes. I feel big anger and big love. It's just all big.

I used to dislike that about me. That everything was BIG.

I've been intentional about walking toward emotional health these past few years. Counseling, whether it's weekly or monthly, has been such an important part of my healing and growth. My counselor and I have talked through some really challenging pains and decisions and I know, no doubt, that I am a better thinker, decision maker, faith person, friend, and romantic partner than I've ever been before. And here's what else is true—the big hasn't gotten smaller. I haven't felt things less. Ten years ago, when I started on this path of really wanting to get some help with my thinking and feeling, I would have thought that going to counseling would make my BIGs smaller. But it hasn't. If anything has changed, it is that the range of my emotions has increased. The depth is the same, but now I can call each emotion by its actual name. But they're all still big.

And I cannot hide that. Sometimes I wish I could. I wish I could tone down what I feel. As I've matured, I have been able to better control my physical and immediate responses, but what I feel is still, well, big. A guy told me once that he knew exactly how I felt about him because I wear my heart on my sleeve. I don't know that he meant it as a criticism, but I'm fairly certain he didn't mean it as a blessing or a compliment. I was scared of that fact for a few weeks, and then I realized that, yes, whether I liked it or not, my heart is absolutely positioned on my sleeve for all to see.

It works to my benefit most days. My friends know I REALLY love them. The people I am with have no question about where I want to be. My favorite stores know it, my favorite restaurants know it; my podcast listeners know it. They know what I love and who I love and what things cycle in and out of my life based on who I'm quoting and what I'm talking about. My heart is on my sleeve because in the truest sense of the phrase, that is just how God made me.

So I love big and I love a lot. In the same way that wisdom sometimes looks like holding back our words, it also sometimes looks like holding back our love—feeling it, yes, but not allowing it to leak out quite so early—whether it's a love for a burrito or a dude. But holding back how much I share doesn't mean I don't feel it. And the more days I live on this planet, the more I am learning that I don't have to control my feelings. They are allowed to ride along with me anywhere I go; they just aren't the best drivers. I need to feel them and hear them and pay attention to them but not let them lead the way.

Love can lead though.

It's powerful to let yourself fall in love with something (or someone). It shows a level of vulnerability when you admit to yourself that the emotion you feel is love. For some reason there's an understanding in Western culture, probably mostly in men but often in women as well, that says we have to hold back our love. Don't get too excited, don't get too into something, be balanced and cool and don't let anyone know how stoked you are. I'm calling a BIG NOPE on that because that's not being wise; that's being scared. Scared to stand out. Scared to tell the truth. Scared to really like something that other people don't really like (that you know of).

You want to learn to have fun? FALL IN LOVE. Fall in love over and over every day with something and maybe someone. Yes, it is going to hurt. But here's the thing about love and vulnerability and saying yes to the big feelings even when they are scary: it makes your heart beat hard and fast. And that's a good reminder that you are not dead. Because you aren't. The thing you thought would kill you did not kill you. You lived. You are living. I hope every time you fall in love with a new pair of shoes or a soccer team or a person who has treated you better than you thought you could be treated reminds you of how very alive you are.

# Onsite

I'VE BEEN IN LOVE with two men in the course of my life, but this guy wasn't one of them. What had started simple and sweet and possible had turned, rather on a dime, to distant and silent and confusing.

Physical distance helped when he went silent. He lives in a completely different region than I do. But the internet is limitless and no number of miles could stop someone from tagging him in a post, thus landing him in my Instagram feed on a fairly regular basis. And honestly, I didn't want to stop seeing his face or reading his words, because I didn't think we were finished. I knew something was very wrong, but I didn't think we were done. I just thought he was being quiet toward me while figuring out what he felt. I thought he was wondering and wrestling and pinning down how we would become us.

I recorded an episode of *Mike Foster's Fun Therapy* podcast the week after the silence started. Mike and I sat together in a recording booth on the south side of town and talked. He knew about this guy, and before we started, I asked him kindly but firmly not to bring up the relationship as it was in a bit of a strange place. I told him that after a few days together in Nashville, the guy had left with no words, and a week later, still no words. And with no real understanding of what was happening or had happened, I didn't want to talk about it.

Mike honored my request, sort of. He indirectly found my wound and pressed on it. Not because he's vicious or manipulative or mean. I think he legitimately did it to show me that there was an injury to be dealt with. Maybe it had to do a bit with my current situation, but it was certainly an older and deeper cut than a man I'd known for such a short time could inflict.

When we finished recording I was a mess of emotions and gripped in pain and tension. The work we had done in that booth was good and right, but it also wrung me out in some deep ways. In a way only a man as kind and loving as Mike Foster could, he leaned forward on the table between us and asked, "Annie, have you ever thought about Onsite? I think you should go."

Many of my friends had been to Onsite. I had heard of it plenty of times, but I had zero desire to go there myself. Onsite is a an emotional-health retreat center that hosts workshops and counseling intensives meant to help you do good hard work on some of the deepest pains in life, the parts of your story you may not have picked but have shaped you and shaped your decision making. That did NOT sound fun to me at all. But I had made myself a promise many years before, when people had first started the conversations about Onsite: if anyone ever SAID I should go, I would. Previously, when people asked if I had been to Onsite before, I would cringe and say nope, expecting the next sentence to be a suggestion that I go. But every time—literally EVERY time before this moment across the table from Mike—the person just moved the conversation forward. So when Mike made the suggestion, I blinked, my heart jumped, and I knew it was time.

I MADE SOME CALLS the next day—to friends who had been to the Living Centered Program (LCP) at Onsite before, to a friend who had recently begun working there, to my business manager to see how we could afford for me to do this. It was November. And by the end of the phone calls, the first week of January was set aside in my budget and my calendar, if not quite yet in my mind and heart. I was going to Onsite.

You gotta know this about me: historically, I do not like pain. I do not like digging too deep into my past because I'm afraid of revealing things that I've forgotten that are painful and better left there—in the past. I worry that there is something that has hurt me but I don't know what it is. So why pick a scab when I don't have to? I recognize this is incredibly backward thinking, but it is how I learned to cope long ago—look away and it will go away. But that's not true. The best course of action is not to ignore; instead, I've learned to always get the sickness out, always sweep the corners, always check the balance in my bank account, always start the hard conversation. But on that day, in that particular time in my life, the idea of sitting in pain and talking about it for a full week (which was my understanding of Onsite) sounded and felt absolutely terrible.

But I also had a feeling.

You know when you KNOW? I'm not speaking of cognitively knowing something; I'm speaking of a deeper knowing. One that may not have words or a proper space in your mind but you know it in the center of you in such a way that it almost feels like too much. I bet not every person experiences knowing quite like this. I think of my podcast episode with author and musician Chris Rice (episode 154) and how differently he experiences the presence of God than I do. But for me, I often know that the Holy Spirit, the very presence of God, is encouraging me or inviting me to something based on this sense I have in the center of me. It also helps that once I have a sense of something God is asking of me, I invite others into it. I do this often, so I did it with Onsite. I went to two mentors and a counselor and two recent Onsite graduate friends and asked for their advice on the opportunity before me. I laid it all in front of each of them. When there was a resounding yes, and my checkbook and calendar were compatible with it all, I had all the confirmation I needed that, yes indeed, the invitation had been from God and was going to work itself all the way through my life.

If I could bring myself to actually go.

I WAS TERRIFIED, for all the reasons listed above. The few early days of the year before my Living Centered Program began, I would burst into tears at the thought of it. I didn't want to be without my phone for a week (lame, but true). I didn't want to leave my friends. I didn't want to sleep anywhere but my own bed. I didn't want to do the work I was afraid was ahead of me. All the silence from the guy, which had become months at that point, had pretty solidly convinced me there was something incredibly wrong with me and I was scared I would finally see the thing, the gruesome truth, whatever it had always been that was keeping me single and causing men (this man, at least) to run away from me without even a handshake and a goodbye.

The day I was supposed to go to Onsite, I packed my things but could not make myself put my RAV4 into drive. Then Heather showed up.

Heather is one of my most faithful friends. She is the one who sees movies with me in the middle of a sad day, and she is the one who will come, do, be when no one else will. She sees without being asked to look and listens far more than she talks, which always makes me feel that she is getting the raw end of this deal (and I am fairly confident it's true).

When she showed up at my house, she handed me a baggie of envelopes. She'd written me a letter for each day I was going to be gone. Then she offered to drive me there. I cried. I was grateful but said no need. I knew what I had to do; I just had to make myself do it. (And to be fully honest, I wanted to have a car at Onsite in case I decided to leave during the week. Having the ability to escape really mattered to me. Hmmmm, sensing a pattern?) So Heather stayed in the driveway with me until I pulled out and pointed my car west. I headed an hour or so outside of the city beside long curves of farmland and sporadic houses and one little hard-to-see sign pointing to Onsite.

I don't want to tell you what happens at Onsite any more than I want to walk you moment by moment through one of my counseling appointments. I'm fine with you knowing the roots of both those needs in my life, but to be fair and loving to myself, what happens behind those closed doors is probably just for me. (And I don't want to ruin your experience if you ever decide to go to Onsite. There are some special moments I want you to have without knowing they are coming.)

My small group leader, Jim Cress, was incredibly insightful, and as we sat around our group room, about ten of us strangers became friends. We shared our stories and worked through some history and by the end of the week, I believed Jim. I believed him when he said I was doing the work to be healthy, and I believed him when he said I was free of the old pains that still tried to tie themselves to me, and I believed him when he said I should be loved well.

He says it to me a lot, actually. Jim and I still keep up on a fairly regular basis, and he still reminds me: "You are so worthy of being chosen by a good, healthy man." He'll say it over lunch or in a text message, and I believe him.

I LEFT ONSITE on a Thursday night after the closing event with all the participants from the program. After a week that had felt far too scary at the beginning, there I was at the end feeling strong and clearheaded. We had barely even talked about the guy who ghosted me—it was never about him, really—but we had walked toward my pain in a new and healing way.

The entire time I was at Onsite, I wore a name tag that read "Annie D" and I carried the key to my room with me wherever I went. That version of myself, Annie D, participated all week, but as we were preparing to leave, I wanted to make some decisions and some promises to myself as just Annie. Always Annie. So I took my name tag off and handed it and my room key to one of my friends. And then, even though it was a very cold evening in January and the sun was already setting, I walked outside.

Through the field along the path at Onsite is a labyrinth created by stones. We had been there once before during the week, but I wanted to visit again alone because I wanted to make some promises to myself. I thought deeply as I wove through the stone path.

Labyrinths are so interesting to me—they weave around the same space, sending you back and forth and back and forth, and you cover four times the amount of ground you should because just going from the start to the finish in a straight line would be so much faster than tracing the maze built for your feet. But it also slows you down, it makes you trust the path and, as they say at Onsite, trust the process.

Once I got to the very center, I looked out over the fields, down the hill, and to the other side of some valley I couldn't see because it was too deep between a few rolling hills. And I said two things out loud, there at the beginning of January:

"God, I want to buy a house by July. And if it would be okay with You, I want to try again."

I really wanted to try again. I wanted a new man to come into my life and with the health that I now had, or at least the health I was going after, I wanted to try again. I never wanted to talk to the guy who ghosted me again; I was strong enough to stop thinking he was better than his behavior. But I wasn't giving up on men or love or big feelings. Because that's how God made me: Always Annie, the girl who loves to love and who wears her heart on her sleeve.

THERE IS REAL POWER to falling in love. I didn't fall in love with that guy, but I can tell you this. My experience with him taught me how to view myself, how to care for myself, how to let those big love feelings grow right here, right inside of me, and direct me in my behavior toward me.

And those two things I said at the center of the labyrinth that last night of Onsite? I did them.

# Harvest House

I ALWAYS PICK a name for the house in which I live. I've never been the girl who names her cars, but I do name my houses.

It may be *Pride and Prejudice*'s fault, with all the Pemberley Manor talk, or maybe it's *Downton Abbey*'s fault, or maybe I should point the finger at Barbie and her Malibu Dream House. Whoever or whatever is to blame, it is just something I do.

The last house I lived in didn't come with a name. In the front yard, three paces off the porch toward the driveway, sat a lamp like the kind you see in C. S. Lewis novels. And of the side panels of glass, two of them were busted out. There was no electricity running out to it, so the lamp never lit up. And when it snowed, or rained, or if the wind blew at just the right speed, the lamp would bend and start leaning toward the ground. (We got a huge snowstorm one winter and that lamp laid ALL THE WAY DOWN on the ground and it was one of the funniest things.)

Quickly my house was named Broke Lamp Manor and there was something mildly profound about that juxtaposition. The regality of naming anything a manor while also having the jankiest lamp in the front yard felt very right and very Annie, particularly in that season of my life.

I GOT HOME to Broke Lamp Manor from Onsite in January and started saving up money. If I'm telling you the total truth, I didn't want to buy a house again as a single woman. I owned a house when I lived in my hometown, and when I sold it, I told myself owning a house as a single woman wasn't for me. I would buy again once I got married, but renting was the life for me. There was so much cost around dealing with the yard and the appliances, and I was in my midtwenties and didn't love all the responsibility that came with owning that house alone. I said over and over again in the decade after selling that house that I wouldn't do it again while single. I would rent until I got married.

I try not to be the person who puts off experiences until I get married and have kids. I mean, some are better put off (ahem), but as far as fun opportunities or open doors, I fear that if I keep waiting, I may never get to do the thing. Travel Europe, jump out of a plane, buy a house. All those things sound incredibly fun and I could miss it all by putting them on the "when I get married" shelf.

For sure I'm as tired of writing about not being married as you are about reading it. But it's still my reality somehow, and it makes me feel a lot of things—grateful and frustrated and proud and disappointed. And I keep finding new things I want to do and want to try and pictures I have for my life that aren't happening. Somehow I'm still supposed to have a great time and call it that publicly to make sure no one thinks I'm desperate. I'm not desperate, but I also don't feel a lot of permission to be sad in the public space about my dreams not coming true. So I try. I just don't let myself save many things anymore, even if my brain screams to write this as a Hallmark movie and only drink hot cocoa out of those mugs with the man I eventually marry versus living my real life right now and making excellent hot chocolate with almond milk and a significant number of marshmallows.

I think that's why that moment at Onsite mattered so much. I knew that buying a house was way more than simply buying a house to me. It was taking one of the few things I had left on the "when I get married" shelf and bringing it down to the "let's just do this now" shelf.

It felt great and terrible at the same time. You get that. I'm sure you have those things too. Even if everything is going very well for you, or if it feels like you've lost everything, there are great and terrible things in your life as well. In that moment at Onsite, I knew it was time to make homeownership a great and terrible reality in my life.

Shannon, my real estate agent and dear friend, helped me house shop in the spring of that year. It took me too long to find the right one, but it was also right on time. I said July while standing in the labyrinth at Onsite, and we ended up closing in June and moving me in on the first day of August. (Also, dear world, why do any of us in the continental United States plan to move in AUGUST? It is so oppressively hot in August, and I cannot pack another house or office and move it in that dreadful month. I feel like I've always and only moved in August, and that is dramatic and not true but it feels like it.)

Shannon and I looked at a billion houses (also dramatic and not true but it feels like it). I liked a handful, but I loved one. But that one, the one by the zoo where I could hear the monkeys at sunset, the one with the little kitchen but the big back porch, that one went to another family who wrote a better letter and made a higher offer than me. So we kept looking, and I never loved one again. In fact, when I saw my current house online, I wasn't sure it was my house. I wasn't sure when I walked through it either. I wanted to be LOVE AT FIRST SIGHT sure, and I just wasn't. I'm a love fast kind of girl, and I wanted to love this house fast. But I didn't. I wanted God to make it incredibly clear and give me some very clear sign when I walked through with Shannon, but it didn't happen like that.

I liked it. The walls were green, I didn't like that. The floor was made of maple-colored wood, I didn't like that either. I liked the house, but, gosh, I wanted to love it.

The timing was right; I knew that. I made an offer that was doable for me and honoring to the homeowner's asking price. I figured if they said yes, this was my house. If they said no, it wasn't.

Spoiler: they said yes. And then I panicked, because it was happening. The little condo was mine. The sentence I had uttered to myself and God out in a field on a freezing cold Thursday a few months before was now really happening. I honestly couldn't believe it. I'm not one to think I can speak something into the universe and so it will be, but I couldn't miss the reality that I had prayed something in January, and here it was in June.

I am surprised when God answers. Isn't that dumb? Why am I so surprised when I ask God for a thing and then He does that thing? I'm wrestling with it now. A few nights ago I asked God to speak into a situation, and then on a DIME the situation changed. I'm living right in the middle of the change I asked God for, and I'm shocked.

Why?

Do I really believe in prayer or not?

I do. I know I do. Deep down in my guts. I keep praying, even when I don't see things change. I just keep sowing into the ground and expecting that someday, far, far from now, I will reap the fruit of my prayers. And I don't question prayer then, when I'm sowing. But when my prayer brings a harvest, I'm surprised.

But God wants me to see this story from Onsite's labyrinth in January to the move-in date in August. He wanted me to feel His nudge, His invitation to pay attention. I can tell it is from Him, guiding my attention toward these details. He's talking a lot to me about harvest.

I WAS MOVED into the condo on the busy street by the stores I love and close to the families I love even more on the first of August. It was a grown-up decision, I knew. I figured out how to balance having fun—because moving into a new place and finding furniture and painting walls and buying far too many throw pillows for my bed is all very fun—with the weight of being responsible for all those decisions. But that feeling I'd been trying to avoid by renting for so many years was back. (Though, to be clear, I bought this particular condo with so much joy because I do not have a yard to care for.

Praise Him!) The walls were all repainted a crisp white, the floors stained a dark and warm color called Jacobean. The only piece of furniture I had was my grandmother's china cabinet. I set out to find a couch and a rug and some stools for the counter between the dining room and kitchen. I couldn't find the right wall to anchor my bed in the master bedroom. I didn't know which drawer would hold the junk, and I couldn't quite sort out where I wanted the plates to go in the kitchen. And what would I put in that hallway closet? During those first few days in the condo, I had more questions than answers and I missed Broke Lamp Manor.

Pretty early into living here, when I asked God what this house was called, I immediately knew it was Harvest House. I saw it written in my heart; I heard it whispered in my guts. And it made sense, still does. He wasn't saying that this house was going to take less work or even that this season of my life would be easier; He was showing me that the work would change. It's no longer sowing work. It's not the digging up and burying seeds kind of work. It's not the waiting and watching kind of work.

It's the answered prayers kind of work.

It's the harvest kind of work.


It took months for me to find the right wall for my bed. I bought a couch and kept it for a year and then traded it out for another one. I've moved my grandmother's china cabinet to three different places in the living room and dining room, trying to find the right spot. Everything is all sorted out kind of fine now. The couch is right. The dining room is right. That tiny bedroom across the hall that I call a library because I want to be fancy and I throw all the books I read in there is still a mess, but it's a real goal to have the room and its closet cleaned and sorted before the end of the year.

Everything has been slow to fall into place, including me. I haven't had a real heartbreak here. I've had small relationships stir up but no real breakups. This house has not held the highest highs or the lowest lows yet. But what has been and what hasn't been in this house is hard to call harvest. The migraines, the bed rest, the lack of falling in romantic love, the fact that the library is still an absolute mess of a room.

It has been a slow falling in love.

I CALLED HEATHER a few weeks into living in the new house, when the fall started to turn cooler. I told her how worried I was that I didn't love this house yet. Staying on budget and feeling at home were in contrast to each other, and budget was winning. But, gracious, did I want to feel at home here.

"My mom says it takes until your first Christmas," Heather said, "and that's when you really feel at home." I didn't know if that could be true, but I knew I would do the best I could to make it so.

I pulled out my Christmas tree and ornaments the second week of November. It was cold and rainy, and it already felt like the holiday season was here. I was going to be traveling a good bit in the upcoming weeks, including that trip to Disneyland, and I would be missing a few weeks of being in my own house. That's what I told people, at least, when I posted on social media about decorating and when I told my real-life friends. But I knew in my heart, I was just grasping to feel at home in a home I owned.

There's a small corner between the dining room and the door to the back porch, right inside the living room, that was perfect for the tree. A little clip of mistletoe hung in the entrance to the kitchen (you can't blame a girl for trying), and the dining room table decor switched from a fall bouquet to a few small decorative Christmas trees. It looked beautiful. Friends came over to eat Christmas treats and watch Hallmark movies, and for the first time, my parents and sister came to town for Christmas Eve and Christmas Day. We made Christmas brunch here, all around the walnut dining room table built by my carpenter friend, Stevie, and we ate on my grandmother's china that cannot go in the dishwasher.

It was different after Christmas; Heather's mom was right. A home warms up when it is decorated for the holidays. I love this line from one of those cheesy Christmas movies: "Anywhere you feel Christmas, you feel home." That was very true at the Harvest House. And the rest of the new year continued, and it was more and more home and more and more of the work of harvesting.

I started to feel at home, and I started to feel in love. And maybe for the first time in my life, I started to see what it looks like to love at a slower pace, moving from like to love. To find the right thing and let it have some time to become right.

That might be a side of harvest and home I didn't know. There must be something about Eden that is slow, that is changing, that is allowed to take time to grow on your soul. Maybe there is a string that ties the work of harvest to slow love, to the lasting kind that burns like coals. It would seem like that's a sowing kind of love. Maybe it's because of my experience in life, but it seems like this slow love I've felt for the Harvest House may harvest more for me than I can even imagine.

# The Little White Kitchen

WHEN I BOUGHT the Harvest House, the kitchen was probably the room I cared about the least. It is little—like a few steps in each direction and you can walk the whole thing little—and all the walls and cabinets are a bright, beautiful shade of white. Even the ceiling is painted white. Above the sink I've hung a sign that says GOOD THINGS ARE COMING. And above the stove, I put a beautiful framed illustration of the Edinburgh skyline with buildings and hot-air balloons. The counters are fake marble but speckled like crazy, which I love. And bizarrely, among all the white cabinets, there is only one with a glass-paneled door. I will never understand why, but I'm also not taking the time or money to change it. The kitchen is lovely and very usable but very small. When I first gave tours of this house to friends, I usually told them, "The kitchen is perfectly Annie-sized—just big enough to reheat something."

I used to like cooking more, back when I made casseroles and soups and full-on meals. But that's when I could eat and serve everything with no concerns about ingredients. That isn't the case anymore.

I'm allergic to cow's milk and cow's milk products. It happened in 2013, my adult-onset allergy's debut appearance, so I had already lived three decades eating cheese dip and pizza and yogurt and ice cream and all the best parts of the world before they were taken away from me.

It's part of having PCOS, polycystic ovary syndrome. Women with this particular disease have to be careful about what they eat, specifically limiting many of the most processed and most delicious things. Something I tell women or married couples often when they talk to me about their own journey with PCOS is that we are actually the lucky ones. Many people are diagnosed with diseases they cannot control, but this one, in many ways, can be controlled by how we treat our bodies.

But listen. It is not fun.

And in a bizarrely devastating way, I've discovered that my body doesn't really like wheat either. I can tell a difference in my shape and my brain and my energy level when I am full of wheat.

But ugh. Bread is fun. It just is. And I'm frustrated.

I'm frustrated about my body's lack of natural health and resilience when it comes to allergies. I'm grateful for a tough immune system and strong bones, but I'm so annoyed at PCOS and annoyed at my reproductive system and annoyed at how some foods cause my body to react negatively.

I've been less disciplined about my wheat intake in the last few months. You want me to get real honest with you? I was super disciplined about wheat when the allergies started in 2013, and I gave it up with a bigger dream in mind. I treated my body really well because it matters a lot for women with PCOS who want to get pregnant. So I lived and ate like a woman on a faith mission. I would do what it took to get my body in tip-top shape for the possibility of babies. But in the last year, I've slacked. I've slacked because I'm older than I was in 2013, and I'm still not married and not interested in having a baby without a spouse. I've slacked because maybe I'm making the choice at this point not to birth a baby myself even though I thought that was something I always wanted. I started eating wheat pretty regularly a few months ago because I got tired of caring about something that may not come to be.

In my most honest moment, I would say living by faith has stopped being fun but eating bread is a lot of fun. And my body is screaming about it. Sometimes God sounds like words and sometimes God sounds like an allergic reaction. Sometimes hearing Him is hearing what my body is saying to me. (I'm not being heretical; I'm just saying I can hear God leading me as I trust what I'm experiencing in my body.)

And I'm new to that. I'm an amateur at that. It isn't fun for me. I'm new at trusting that my body is telling me something and trusting that God wants me to notice too.

The thing I have to decide today (and decide again tomorrow and every day after) is if I love my future more than I love my present. Can I think past where we are this minute, the fun that would come from food RIGHT NOW, and think about my future?

WE DON'T TALK about body stuff on the podcast much. That's partly because it tends to feel so deeply personal to me but also because I really don't want to do anything, or host any conversation, that would lead a man or a woman to believe that their body is wrong. We get pitched so many diet books, food books, fitness coaches, all of it, and I almost always say no.

Because I don't want to have conversations that make my friends on the other side of the recording, the listeners on their commute or folding their laundry or on their treadmill, wonder if they should feel shame for how they are living when it comes to their own body. That's not my job, that's not my goal, and I don't want to be a part of anyone feeling any level of shame.

In fact, my listeners probably hear me talk more about loving your body right here, right now than anything else. I want to have conversations like the one I had with Mandisa (episode 171). I want to sit and talk about how we feel about our bodies, how we are handling our feelings and our time of exercise and the loud things we hear in our heads. I want THOSE conversations, not a coach telling me that I need to count something or buy some new tool or measuring cup. I'm just not here for that.

And I want to have conversations with chefs. I love people who love food, who think about their meal before they make it, who use the exact right ingredients and create recipes for us.

I love Food Network shows, but I've never been a huge fan of those cooking competitions that everyone else loves. Mostly because—again, thanks, dairy allergy—I know I'm not going to try to make any of the foods they make on the shows. And I'll never get to be a judge, though I think it would be incredibly fun. And I'm jealous I can't cream together butter and sugar and mix it with a pile of flour in my own kitchen, if I'm being honest. But for some reason, I got hooked on Food Network's *Spring Baking Championship*. It was on television when I was on bed rest for the migraines, so I pretty much fell in love with it. But there was one particular chef I liked the most. Cory Barrett.

There was always something about the way Chef Cory baked that felt deeper and more profound than just the making of cakes and candies. That may sound silly, but that's how it felt. Like every dessert he made, everything he baked, wasn't enough to him if it looked good or tasted good. It had to be precise, it had to be beautiful, it had to have meaning and bring him as much joy making it as it would bring the judges when they were eating it. I think it just always felt like he was having fun. Pretty early in the competition, I found myself rooting for Chef Cory. He was the tallest contestant, he had a very good mustache, and he always talked about his wife and kids. He seemed like the kind of guy I would want to be friends with, or the kind of guy I would like to tell people about, saying, "Yeah, we were friends in college. I'm so excited for where his life has gone." Know what I mean?

If I was out of town when a new episode released, it would be the first thing I'd watch when I got home. And I was constantly cheering for Chef Cory. He stressed me out once when he got in the bottom three, but don't worry—he didn't get eliminated that week. In fact, he never got eliminated. Sorry to spoil it for you, but he won. The guy I had been cheering for from day one was the winner of season five's *Spring Baking Championship*.

I cheered. I literally stood up in front of my television during the final judging and had my arms crossed like my favorite football team was on the three-yard line about to score a touchdown. Then when he won, I cheered like a crazy person in my own home.

A few days later, I got real brave and tweeted at Chef Cory. I asked him if he would be willing to come on the podcast and talk about winning. (Listen, I'm never going to be the one who says no for someone else. I'll always let them say no for themselves.) But a bit to my surprise, he responded and said he'd love to be on the show.

We went back and forth trying to find a recording date and finally got it locked in. And then I panicked. What would I even ask him?!? "Uh, great job winning that contest. . . . Was it cool?" I could just totally see myself bombing this interview. But you know the show rules—the only guests welcome are friends and people I wish I were friends with, so I switched my mindset. This wasn't just a guy I'm a huge fan of, this was a guy whom I already thought would be fun to be friends with. The interview was a chance to give it a go.

Chef Cory's episode (episode 146) will long remain one of my favorites. He was exactly the same guy in our conversation as he was on the show. To me, that's the highest sign of integrity—when you experience the same person being the same person in multiple environments. Chef Cory was just as fun as I figured he would be. We learned all about the behind-the-scenes details of the competition and how he got into cooking and baking, and then he said a sentence that I have repeated multiple times and that has stuck with me personally. "Lots of people say food is medicine, but I would say cooking is medicine."

Wow. I needed to hear that.

Even though he didn't mean to and couldn't have known me well enough to know how much I needed to hear that, Chef Cory was preaching something important to me.

I have been living for years with the mantra "food is medicine." I've said it to others and to myself ad nauseam. Food will heal, food will heal, food will heal. Eat the right foods and your body will heal. But cooking as medicine? Maybe that's an Eden I didn't know I had lost. But when I heard it existed, I missed it.

So I started cooking a little bit more. (Don't get it twisted, I'm not your new favorite food blogger, but I am using my kitchen for more than reheating these days.) I pulled out all of Danielle Walker's cookbooks, the family cookbook my mom put together a few years ago, and a few others I had stacked around the house. And I began to make soup. Lots of different soups and stews. It's my favorite method of getting meat and vegetables into my body. I used the stove and the Crock-Pot and the Instant Pot. I made small one-person servings of soup and big pots that ended up in my freezer and fridge and in a few containers delivered to friends' houses as well. I made soups that went great and one that was far too spicy for me so it all got delivered elsewhere.

Then the fun started as I began to experiment with changing up the recipes a bit to fit my own taste. Would I like this one better if the vegetables were roasted first? What if I swapped out sweet potato for white potato? (Amateur tip: don't.) I've now perfected a few soups for myself that stay in a pretty constant rotation in my fridge and freezer. (The leftover roasted chicken and vegetable soup from Danielle Walker[1] and the one-pot pumpkin black bean soup from Minimalist Baker are two I make on repeat.[2] But I make them without the peppers because SPICY. You've been warned.)

And in a way that I don't know how to explain to you just like I didn't know how to explain it to my counselor, cooking started to heal me. It didn't heal or change my body, but after weeks of cooking in my kitchen, the way I talked about and thought about and looked at my own body changed drastically. It's like everything just settled. The waves of self-hate that had been crashing on my shore at a high-tide pace went back out to sea as I stirred and chopped and roasted and waited. Love grew as I waited—love for my kitchen and for my house and for myself and for the way God made food for us to eat. What I thought I was gaining in better food and faster service by eating out and having food delivered, I was losing all along in healing.

So I'm usually in my kitchen two nights a week or so, making one thing or another. (Well, until an unforeseen global pandemic struck the world, closing all restaurants and canceling all dinners with friends. COVID-19 had me in my kitchen EVERY night.) Sometimes it's a soup if my stash is running low. Though, to be honest, it never runs low. When I get down to about two servings left in the freezer, I get to scheming which soup will be next. But I've also gotten in the habit of making egg salad, a mixture that you either love or hate, and if you love it, you love it a very certain way. I made up my recipe—six eggs, about 1/3 cup of mayonnaise, 1/4 cup of mustard, 1 tablespoon of dried dill, and one chopped pickle. You will probably hate that particular recipe, so adjust it to what you want. But I keep a container of this deliciousness around most of the time. (This book has literally been fueled by Pamplemousse La Croix, egg salad, and sporting events on television in the background.) I also made an attempt at boiled peanuts in my Instant Pot this week, but they were subpar for sure. I'll give it another go soon enough.

But the point is, I'm having fun in my kitchen—something that hasn't happened in a long time. Since the days of baking cakes and making chicken and dumplings and doing all the southern cooking that includes all the dairy and all the wheat. I am being healed. Cooking is fun and cooking is the medicine that is bringing me back to a pure love I haven't known in a long time.

# Lost Valley Ranch

IT'S WEIRD TO PLAN a vacation as a single person. You can get your crew of friends together, but making sure everyone is on the same budget and on the same schedule is no small task. It can be incredibly fun, but it can also be incredibly challenging. You can go alone. I have friends who love that. But that's not going to be the epitome of a good time for me. I can go to a movie alone just fine, but going on a cruise alone or to Boston for a week by myself doesn't work for me.

A few years ago, I just didn't vacation. I took days off from work, calling it a "staycation," but I mainly slept in and played with my friends' kids and ignored my emails. (I do those three things at some point in a normal week if all is well, so it really wasn't that outside of my non-vacation life.)

A few of us sat around dinner one night in the winter, all single men and women, and we talked about how finding the right vacation without a spouse or kids can be so challenging. How the money is never easy to set aside even though we all follow Instagram accounts about the best vacation spots and we get all the tips on how to vacation on the cheap. How there are places we want to see, trails we want to hike, meals we want to eat, sporting events we want to attend, but it all seems out of reach for one reason or another.

I watch my friend Barrett do it really well. His crew of friends seems to see all the places and go to all the games and experience all the experiences and have all the fun, but then I remember that he WORKS IN TOURISM so yeah, it makes sense. But I'm still jealous.

ONE OF MY FAVORITE married couples, Jenn and Rhett, texted me in mid-April to see if I was free to join them for a week of vacation. They were spending the second week of July at Lost Valley Ranch, a Colorado Dude Ranch experience tucked in the Rocky Mountains, and they thought I might enjoy it as well. Their offer felt like a deep exhale. And while I had never been to Lost Valley Ranch before, many of my friends had, and the owners are friends of mine as well. Any chance to go to Colorado in the summer sounds fun to me because I deeply love Colorado in the summer.

I experienced it for the first time as a teenager when my dad had a CPA Convention in Colorado Springs in June. I fell in love immediately (this doesn't shock you, I know). The height of the mountains, the green of the trees, the warm weather that is enjoyable to be out in but isn't ruin-your-life-or-your-clothing-level-hot. And then there is just something about Colorado, about the idea of the Wild West. Westward Expansion has been one of my favorite genres of books or shows for a long time. There's something that feels brave and historic about those mountains, knowing that people crossed them in a time when it wasn't a casual or easy venture.

Heading to Lost Valley Ranch that July was one of those vacations that started out terrible. You know the ones. My flights were messed up, my rental car was hit by a teenager in the parking lot of a Starbucks seconds after I tasted my drink and thought, *Ew, that isn't right*. Cell service was spotty at best and I have absolutely no sense of direction, so I was nervous and stressed as I followed written instructions and gripped the steering wheel with all my might on my two-hour drive from the airport to the mountains. (Jenn and Rhett offered to pick me up, but I had romantic notions of stopping along the way and taking pictures so I wanted to drive myself. Bad move. I won't do that next time.) There was nothing relaxing about my first day in Colorado, and by the time I got to the ranch, I was frazzled in every way. And out of place. And so tired. Tired from waking up for a 5:00 a.m. flight but also tired from a week of preaching at a summer camp, tired from preaching the day before at my church, and tired from six months of really hard work. (There's this saying "When you have your dream job, you'll never work a day in your life," and that is so laughable because I have pretty close to my dream job and I have never worked harder. Can I get an amen from the rest of y'all living on mission and on purpose? Sheesh. We are a tired people.)

But this was supposed to be vacation, right?

I know myself pretty well. The feeling I had standing in the lobby of Lost Valley Ranch was a mixture of exhaustion, feeling out of place, and hangriness. Jenn had saved me a salad, so I sat with her at a table and ate it quickly before immediately requesting a nap. I knew a nap would help, but there was a deeper unsettled feeling in me that a few minutes or hours of sleep wasn't going to fix.

That night, a room full of strangers sang "Happy Birthday" to me, and they brought me a gluten-free, dairy-free chocolate cake. It was delicious, but I still felt a bit awkward because everyone else had already been together for a day and here I was a day late and people were singing to me, a virtual stranger. I smiled and said thank you, and we ate the cake. Then we walked outside for a social hour kind of thing with the rest of the guests at the ranch.

It was beyond beautiful. The weather was cool enough that short sleeves were comfortable but so were long sleeves. The sun was setting slowly, and the sky was lighting up with shades of pink and orange and moments of bright red. And there was a charcuterie board that had the most beautiful assortment of cheeses and meats and crackers and honey. I LOVE HONEY ON A CHARCUTERIE BOARD!

But for some reason I felt uncomfortable in my own skin. It was partly due to the elevation making my body feel bloated, but it was also partly that being me had been hard lately. It's the same story you already know. Loving myself is the hardest task God has given me, and while I am significantly better at it today than I was twenty, ten, and five years ago, I still have some deep and low days.

I thought everyone at the ranch knew me, knew Annie F. Downs. It's a weird part of my job, but in my current life, if there is a group of Christians in their twenties and thirties, I can usually correctly assume that someone in there recognizes me for my work. I am super fine with that and really enjoy it, actually, but it changes my eyes on vacation. And that's okay, it changes my eyes on everything. It just reminds me to say to myself, *Someone is probably watching. Someone is probably listening. Make sure you are who they think you are.* It's not that I am two different people—a public Annie and a private Annie—it's just that I know I'm expected to be smiley and happy and funny and to ask a lot of questions. And that is me, don't get me wrong, but on days when I don't feel all that, it doesn't matter. I choose to be that version of Annie because I want everyone who meets me for the first time in person to get the Annie they expect. I was doing that at the dinner, and at the charcuterie board, and as I met the staff and other guests at Lost Valley, but something felt off about it. I couldn't read the people. Did they care or not? Did they have an expectation or not? Why did I feel so uncomfortable not knowing?

It happens to all of us when we walk into rooms, doesn't it? We scan the room, wonder who THEY want us to be, whoever the THEY is, and then we decide if we're going to be who THEY want. I'd like to think I'm the girl who shows up just as I am, but THEY often want me to be me and show up as me, so somehow even me being me can turn into me being who they want. Phew, I'm tired.

Maybe that was it. Maybe I was just tired, maybe I needed rest. Maybe I was putting too much hope in that vacation. Do you ever do that? Sometimes when I do get a few days off or go on vacation, it feels like I gather up all my worries and concerns, thinking I can dump them on vacation like a bag of trash down a chute in a high-rise apartment building in Chicago. But that wasn't happening. The things I was feeling about myself and my life weren't in a bag headed far away from me. They were with me at all times. And the combined confusion over not knowing who they wanted me to be, my body being out of sorts and out of size and out of favor with me, and my exhaustion from the first half of the year, made me wish I could disappear.

YOU CAN GET SO LOST in your own life and your own expectations that you forget what it is like to be just a person. You're not just a mom or a dad, you're a person. You're not just a teacher, you're a person. You're not just his girlfriend, you're a person. You're not just her fiancé, you're a person. You're not just your job or your calling or your ministry or your relationships, you are a person.

And if you don't remember that you are a person first—that when it was just Eden, you were just you—then fun may be easy to find, but it will be hard to maintain. It had been such a slippery slope for me that by the time I made it to the ranch, I didn't realize my person-ness was lost in my public-ness.

But then we ate breakfast on Wednesday.

Jenn and I sat down with our friend Tony, who runs the ranch, over at his table in the back corner, where he usually sits alone and reads the news on his iPad. We ordered breakfast and the special was my favorite of the whole week: chilaquiles. It is corn tortilla strips with beans poured on top with fried eggs, green salsa, and cheese and sour cream as well (if you aren't allergic to dairy). As my plate arrived, Tony took his glasses off, placed his hands on the table, and looked at me. "You've got to quit doing the thing you're doing. You're not supposed to do that here." My eyes were probably as big as saucers. I didn't think I knew what he meant, but something in me did know. I felt the stir in me, that he was saying something very true, but I didn't quite know what yet. He continued looking right at me. "You don't have to be anything for anyone here. Quit doing that."

And then I knew.

I was uncomfortable in my skin because my skin was tough and this place told me to be soft. I was struggling to find my footing because the ground was meant for me to be barefoot, and I wouldn't take off my public life shoes for fear of how my bare toes would look to this world.

For an Annie who prides herself on being true and vulnerable and exactly the same woman in person that you meet online, I had begun to morph person Annie into public Annie instead of the other way around.

We can all do it. We can all take the THING we are and after some practice and some time and some wounds and some worries, we can surely turn the THING into WHO we are. Mom. Musician. Friend. Boss. Pastor. Your thing becomes you, and when you find yourself in a soft place, like Lost Valley Ranch or a conversation with a trusted friend or even time alone with your Bible and journal, it feels uncomfortable because it just doesn't sit well with the tough skin you've acquired. And I had done that. I had done that in some really quiet and slow ways so that podcast listeners couldn't hear and friends couldn't see and I didn't know until Tony said it.

And then I really knew.

I knew in the crying-at-breakfast kind of way. Suddenly my eyes were full of tears and I couldn't see clearly because I was seeing myself so clearly. I don't know how Tony knew things about me that I didn't even totally know or how he knew them so quickly. Maybe he sees a lot of thick-skinned folks come through the cow gate of Lost Valley Ranch, or maybe he just saw me. But he was very right.

I spent that day, and the next day, peeling back the skin that was too tough, and I started relaxing. I had already been napping every single day (a vacation must for me), but I started resting in my soul after that breakfast—when I knew Tony saw what I couldn't see or didn't want to see, when I realized it wasn't too late to fix it.

I can always have fun, I can always find it and chase it and create it, but wow it was something different when I felt like a person again. When I felt the simplicity of Annie being enough. Not Annie F., not Annie the podcaster or Annie the author or Annie the friend who does Instagram stories. Just Annie. I had lost her for a bit in the hubbub of the rest of my life, which seems really possible for a lot of us in our jobs or relationships, but then I found her. Well, Tony found her.

WHAT I WANT to write next is "And then the rest of vacation was magically magical and isn't that neat!" But it didn't go down like that in my heart. I still struggled, I still hurt, I still had moments. I can think of one particularly rough moment outside the barn under twinkly lights, when I just wanted to be invisible. I was barely wearing any makeup that week—that's part of vacation for me—and I had seen a picture of me that just did not live up to Annie F. Downs's standards for what I want posted (gross thinking, I know). But I knew it wasn't my picture or my feed, so it wasn't my say, and that bothered me.

But there was this one other moment that trumped them all. It happened in that same room where Tony had given me the what-for half a week earlier. On the last afternoon of your first week at Lost Valley Ranch, you create a design, like a cattle brand, and the wranglers burn it into the wood in the dining room—on either the ceiling or one of the walls. And for years to come, as you spend more weeks there in the summer, a wrangler will add a check mark beside your brand. Creating your brand is a big deal because it lasts for years and years. There are some family brands that have over twenty check marks, indicating decades of vacations shared at Lost Valley Ranch.

I wanted an A and an F. I didn't want the D because my thinking and hope is it won't always be my last initial, but the A and the F aren't going anywhere. Jenn is a graphic designer so she mocked up a few things for me on a napkin at breakfast that morning, and one of them caught my eye. There is a line down the center, like a tent pole. To the left a line leans up against the tent pole, then another crosses them, creating the A. Then to the right of the tent pole, that horizontal line of the A continues to make the top line of the F. Then a shorter line finishes it. It's simple and profound and beautifully illustrates the first two initials of my name.

My favorite wrangler, Tall Johnny from New York who has a mustache and likes riddles, said he would burn my brand into the wooden ceiling. That felt very right. We placed it right next to Jenn and Rhett's, around those of some other friends of ours who frequent Lost Valley Ranch but weren't with us that particular week. And that also felt so right. I watched as Johnny climbed the ladder, traced my design with a pencil, then went and grabbed a hot iron brand and started going over the pencil lines with hot metal that burned through the wood. And there I was, no makeup on my face, hair pulled back in a lazily made ponytail, wearing a pink tank top that says "Hello Summer" and black yoga pants and my Nikes, with tears coming to my eyes. I had done it. I had peeled off the part of me I didn't know I had worn in. It felt like a profound moment. We weren't leaving yet, but it was the crossing of some sort of finish line to me.

Jenn captured a picture of that moment. I'm looking up at the brand, so freshly burned on the ceiling that we could still smell it, and I'm smiling with a tear in the corner of my eye. Tall Johnny is standing beside me, hands on his hips, looking down at me and smiling the sweetest friend smile in the world. His eyes seem proud of how happy I am with his work. And that picture tells a really fun story. The truth of a person who left her "brand" at a breakfast table across the room a few days earlier so she could just be the person again.

# New York Tattoo Company

THAT SAME JENN has become one of my best friends in the last few years. Not only does she let me vacation with her and her husband but she has also walked with me through all kinds of relationships. She and I have talked through friendship situations and work problems. She's listened to me share my excitement about a new romance and sat with me when I poured out my fears about whether or not a new guy was right for me. And through the ebbs and flows, the ups and downs, she's repeatedly said the same phrase to me: "Savor this."

On my best days, when a guy I'm dating is being incredibly sweet and exactly the kind of dude I'm looking for, she'll say, "Isn't that great? Savor this. Don't rush it. This is the good stuff." And she is right. At the same time, on the days that feel confusing or a guy is being quiet and the panic starts to rise up in me, she'll say it again, "Savor this. There's something to be learned here. Something to be healed. You should sit in it." And although I want to escape the pain, like a snake trying to get out of its skin, I know she's right. Even if that pain leads to pure sadness, Jenn asks me if I'm willing to savor that too.

I'm not great at that. When a relationship ends, I give myself a day or two to cry, but then the voice in my head changes from being a comforting friend to a motivational coach. I tell myself it's time to stop feeling sad. *It's up and to the right from here on out, Downs! Time to move on to someone or something or someplace new! Go do something fun!* But Jenn doesn't always agree with that, and I'm grateful.

I'm learning. A little while back, after a man and I decided to end things, when I normally would have made myself believe all should be well, I was still choosing to savor the sadness, to experience it and call it that. I was still very sad, but I didn't make myself do anything about it. I got to work and for some reason two of my friends who are on staff at church, Ashley and Mike, were the only people in the office. (At the time, my office was in the creative team section of the church office space. So while I had my own room that had a door that closed, the best part was having some of my favorite people, my church's creative team, just outside the door.) I walked over to Ashley and tears were in my eyes before I could even stop them. She grabbed my hand and we sat down, right there on the floor, right at the edge of the bank of desks where Mike sits. And then Ashley said, "I need to lie down," so there we were, backs on the floor, side by side, her right hand holding my left hand, tears streaming out of the corners of my eyes, Mike in his desk chair right beside us.

It felt holy. I can't explain it. But something about the childlikeness of just lying on the floor, something about being with these two friends who have walked almost a decade of life with me, something about being allowed to keep crying when my brain told me I wasn't allowed to anymore, it just all felt holy and connected. I kept thinking, *Savor this moment. It matters.*

So often in our world today, no matter if your personality is just like mine or totally different, we think strength is shown when we force sadness to end. We think we have grown up, matured, and increased in health and humanness when we put a full stop to feeling sad or disappointed. Pulling ourselves up by our bootstraps is always rewarded. But it just wasn't ever meant to be that way. We rush seasons in our personal lives, hurrying through dating for engagement, hurrying through college to get to adulthood, hurrying through the toddler years to get to kindergarten, hurrying through the chemo to get the clear diagnosis. But what is there to gain from letting the season decide its own length instead? No amount of self-control, willpower, or changing your wardrobe is going to make the summer turn to fall fast enough for some of us. Fast enough for me.

So even in August, when the sun is hotter than you want it to be, and as September approaches and "Surely we get to wear fall clothes in North America now, right?"—we need to remember we actually have no control of that. We notice the mornings that start to have a bite of coolness in the air, we love the nights when we have to grab a cardigan or a jacket on the way out the door to dinner. But we have no control over any of it. We just get to notice it, enjoy it, and savor it.

I HAVE A couple tattoos. (I've told you in detail about the first two in my book *Looking For Lovely*.) The decision to go from zero tattoos to one tattoo was massive and took years of prayers and counsel and way too many thoughts to get me there. But going from one to two or two to three, is significantly (and possibly concerningly) easier.

The first one, a simple cursive script of the word *grace* in my friend Molly's handwriting is on my left wrist, and when I see it, I remember to be kind to myself. The second one, on my right arm, is in my buddy Connor's handwriting, reminding me not to give up—*persevere*, it says—and I sometimes rub my thumb over it like a rosary when I need a reminder to hang in there. They are both white ink, and on my very pale shade of white-girl skin, they practically look like brands.

And ever since that day, lying on the floor crying with Ashley and Mike, I have known I wanted *savor this* as my next tattoo. But listen, I'll tell you what I DID NOT want is a tattoo connected at all with any particular dude or any particular relationship ending. So I knew I needed to wait a while to make sure the phrase stuck around in my life and continued to be true for a few seasons on the calendar before I permanently marked it on my body.


I HAVE SUCH a proclivity to rush out of THIS and into THAT. I just don't sit in the middle of things very well, even the things I love most. I love soccer but I sometimes find myself wishing for the final game of the World Cup while the first game is being played, simultaneously feeling sadness that since the tournament I've been anticipating has now started, that means it will end. (I'm a complicated woman, y'all.)

But as I continued to practice what it looks like to savor things, I never wavered. It felt so deep inside me, it was a part of me. So when I was planning a trip to New York City, a city I connect with on a lot of levels, at a pivotal season change for me personally, I knew it was the right time. I asked Jenn to write out the phrase in her handwriting, much like Molly and Connor had done for me with the other two tattoos. But as the day got closer, something in me shifted. I wanted to see my own handwriting telling me to "savor this."

I was heading to New York to hang with Ginna Claire and Mary Kate. These two women who toured through Nashville as part of the cast of *Wicked* became two of my best friends after the show packed up and moved to another theater in another town.

I had booked a flight to the city for a few days to see them, to eat ramen, and to write. I love writing in New York; there's just something about the buzz and the hubbub and the way the city never sleeps (or even gets quiet) that absolutely puts juice in my creative booster. Looking back, I can pick out the pieces of my work that have the stamp of being written in New York. Even if I don't exactly remember, I can feel the cadence and the intentionality around the words.

I mentioned to the girls that I might want another tattoo, and Mary Kate wanted one as well. So we made a plan that Friday morning before Ginna Claire, who was no longer the touring Glinda but the Broadway Glinda instead, had to be at the Gershwin Theater for the matinee. Mary Kate and I made appointments at a recommended tattoo parlor, I drew out exactly how I wanted it to look and, in the end, I combined my handwriting with Jenn's. SAVOR is mine; THIS is hers.

And it feels absolutely perfect because of how we've walked through life together the last few years.

Then later that day, right at dinnertime, Mary Kate and I showed up for our appointments. The tattoo didn't take very long, but it hurt VERY MUCH INDEED. Dean, the artist, was as compassionate as a tattoo artist should be, which is to say a little but not too much because I was literally getting two words in pretty small font on the center of my left forearm, not a massive eagle across my whole back.

The buzzing started and I wasn't allowed to clench my fist because the muscle had to stay soft. So as he was needling all up and down my forearm, I was definitely in pain. And sweating. And using my other hand to grip my thigh tightly. I felt like I could barely handle it, and then I remembered exactly what he was permanently affixing to my arm—SAVOR THIS. I started thinking through what that meant in this scenario. What did it mean to savor this very pain I was experiencing? To call this fun because it's something so different and special. To stay in it, to appreciate it, knowing it will never happen again just like this. To slow my breathing, slow my rushing heart and mind, and just be in the moment while I was getting a tattoo. So I tried. I kept saying to Mary Kate, "We are the lucky ones. This is what we get to do on a Friday night." And I would continue to list ways we were lucky, even through gritted teeth. I would look Dean in the face, when I thought the pain was going to be so much that I would have to ask him to stop, and instead I would thank him. I would say out loud how grateful I was he was available to do this thing that was bringing me pain that I had volunteered for. I told him how thankful I was for his skill and his time and how much I loved what was happening. I did all I could to sit in the moment and realize it was unique, it was special, and it was—if I wanted it to be—a memory to be had with God.

I felt so loved right there in the New York Tattoo Company, this long skinny store off the main thoroughfare with just a couple of tattoo chairs, fluorescent lighting, and walls covered in photos of past work and sketches of possible tattoos. It's not that I felt loved by Dean, per se, though I think we are definitely friends by now. But I felt very loved by Mary Kate, who stood by me and videoed moments of the process and told me how brave I was. I felt so loved by God, who had orchestrated so many things to align at just the right time and just the right place with just the right people to be able to get this tattoo. So many details had to fall into place for that moment to happen. But there isn't anything about happenstance or things simply falling into place in the kingdom of God. It's all handled. It's all aligned. It's all a gift. And God does that a lot, it seems. When I look for His hand in the stories that I'm living, I always seem to find Him.

But I also felt so loved by me. I was behaving with such kindness and courage. I was honoring myself and the strength that lives in me by getting the tattoo I had long wanted and sitting in the pain of it. I was doing what reminded me of the best parts of myself.

I'm working on falling in love with myself. I know that may sound weird unless you love Lizzo like I do and then you KNOW that you're your own soul mate. But for too long, I've decided that how I feel about me is based on how *you* feel about me. Or more honestly, how he feels about me, whoever the current "he" is. I know it probably sounds a bit

New Age-ish to you, to work on the love I feel for myself, but I just have to. The lack of it has become somewhat toxic for me. Well, more than somewhat. Significantly toxic is a better descriptor.

I talked with Jenn recently about how I have to change how I view myself. And it's not a problem that a marriage or a man will fix. Because I know that my insecurities while trying to find a man will not disappear upon acquiring one; they will simply shape-shift. It may look like new iterations or sound like new questions, but it will be the same old toxins. New bottle, same poison.

So moments like getting my tattoo—when I am fully present in my body, in my pain, and in kindness to myself—are proof that I'm not drinking the poison today.

# Ryman Auditorium

Some of the things I love, like the Ryman Auditorium, I'm going to love forever.

And while that may not change, I do. I live in the Harvest House. I am healthier in body and heart than I've been in a long time. There's a really kind single man who seems to enjoy getting to know me (and I feel the same about him). And in all those ways, I am different.

I am loving better than I've ever loved.

But I find myself wanting to write a chapter of this book about the Ryman Auditorium, because of what it meant to see Drew Holcomb perform there once again. And I'm laughing because I write about the Ryman in every single one of my books.

And I know me. I'm going to love that room forever, and I am here to tell you the most fun in life comes from loving what you love and letting yourself love all the way in and withholding only when wisdom says to, not when fear is speaking. Yet I'm embarrassed to write about the Ryman again, but there is just something about the way that place holds me. It's not possible, and I roll my eyes even as the words cross my mind, but it feels like the Ryman loves me too. Like it's home in some ways.

What is it about the Eden I've lost that I find there?

CONNOR AND I sat at breakfast this morning, sitting in eight years of friendship, and we talked about some new decisions he's been making and the filters he is using. I've watched him grow from a college dude to a man, and life just isn't as easy for him (or me) as it was eight years ago. It made me sad to look across the table at this man who is no longer a boy. This man who has experienced some deep hurts and real wounds that have told him EDEN IS LOST. His frame is the same as when we met. He is still a muscular, tall, athletic man, but the simple days aren't in his eyes anymore. The tenderness that came from trusting has been replaced with an understanding. And nothing is sadder than that understanding, the one that settles deep into your insides, the understanding of how the world works. An understanding that the search for Eden is current and urgent and sometimes disappointing.

But even as I listened to him, I didn't want him to live any different. I didn't want to grab his face and yell "LOVE ANY-WAY! GO FOR IT! DO NOT BE SCARED!" Instead, I said, "Yeah, this is sad but this is growing up and it's just part of it." I pretty much told him it's time to search for Eden. But I'm worried there are places he is leaving, where he won't go back, because the understanding has told him the search is not worth the effort.

SOMETIMES THE SEARCH for Eden is going to require new places, new friends, new experiences. The fun of jumping out of an airplane is something most people only experience once. But there's always a chance to come back to the places where you felt love before.

That can go sideways. I know. I went on a date at my very favorite restaurant and while that date was great, the relationship wasn't. And in ways, though it was a safe and sacred and favorite place, chock-full of great memories from years of time spent around the tables, there was a scar upon it after that relationship ended. And I had a choice. I could never go there again. I could let that be the very last time I ever crossed the threshold of the Loveless Cafe. But a life without those biscuits and country ham is not a life I want to live. And I'm just not okay with giving away places that I deeply love.

That decision—"I will not leave that place in my memory"—is one made with the understanding in place. It was a decision that took courage and willingness. It was an adult decision with a childlike view of the way the world could work, even if it doesn't always.

Because there are places that are lost forever, like my childhood home, so shouldn't we go back to the ones that we can? Even if it hurts?


I ALMOST LOST the Ryman once.

I was in a section I never sit in anyway, so I should have known. The musician onstage, the one I bought a ticket to see, he and I have a complicated relationship. He doesn't know that, of course, I just know it. I know it because the music from one of his albums walked every cobblestone street of Edinburgh, Scotland, with me when I lived there a few years ago. His music has since changed direction a bit, and while I was excited to see him live, I knew a new album had released and my guess was it would be a night of new music much more than the album that had meant so much to me.

There was a man in the audience, a man who had bought one ticket by himself and was sitting by himself, a few sections to the right of me. And he and I were in a complicated relationship as well. The difference is he knew it too.

I spent the whole show worrying about him, the man a few sections over, and worrying about the music, from the man onstage, and wondering why it all felt off to me. I wanted the old understanding we had. I wanted the old album that the musician had created that was such a good friend to me in a foreign city. And I wanted to be in that old life, the one across the ocean with the people across the ocean, because I wasn't worried like this there.

But in that moment, things were off. And it all fell apart with the man in the other section the next day. It fell all the way apart.

Somehow I knew that was going to happen the night before at the Ryman. I kept thinking about it as the music played. And I didn't know how I'd go back there, to my favorite room in Nashville, because when it was all said and done, something was taken from me that night that I was never going to get back.

WHEN DREW HOLCOMB first came to my office to record the podcast episode that would release the same week as his album *Dragons* (episode 160), I forgot to hit record on his microphone. He sat down across the table from me and I hit record on the machine but forgot to fire up his microphone specifically. So after we talked deep and wide for an hour, none of the material was usable.

He's a gracious man. When I called and told him that we would need to do the show again, he quickly made it fit into his schedule. When he arrived at my office, I had a bottle of Belle Meade Bourbon awaiting him because, my word, who agrees to do the same podcast conversation twice?

But the second time was actually better. Way better. And we talked about our experiences at the Ryman Auditorium. And it just seems true, for me as an audience member as well as for Drew as an artist, that this place holds something special.

I travel and speak in places a lot as part of my job. I've been in hundreds of churches over the last seven years. Some I can call to mind immediately and tell you a story about my time there. Some I remember when I walk through the door and see familiar faces or rooms. Some, I'm sorry to say, escape me altogether until my memory is jogged by a friend.

A week after our second podcast recording, Drew was playing the Ryman. I bought two tickets and a friend and I went and sat in section 15, row B.

I didn't realize how close I felt to losing the Ryman until I listened to Drew sing and realized that room still had a place in my heart. It had been years since I thought about the scar on the Ryman Auditorium, but it had also been a while since I deeply cared about an experience there. I had been to shows between the two, but I couldn't tell you who played or who went with me to the concerts. In all that time, there isn't a show that totally stands out, except the one where I stood on the stage.

IN BETWEEN THE SHOW when I thought I lost the Ryman and the show where I knew it was found again, I got to stand onstage for the first time ever. My friend Dave Barnes did a concert and comedy show, and afterward, when the only people left in the room were our friends and a few ushers shooing us out, I walked from the back of stage left and up to the front of the stage. All the lights were up in the lower level and in the balcony. The room felt totally empty; the stained glass windows in the back were dark. But it didn't matter. It was so special.

As I stood on that stage, I scrolled through my memories of the best shows I had seen there. There were many moments etched in my memory so much deeper and truer than that night that left a scar. When Mumford & Sons played the room, the first time Dave Barnes headlined, when Ingrid Michaelson sang "Somewhere Over the Rainbow," and when Ira Glass performed a live podcast. Secret Sisters once spun the room with their harmonies, and The Belonging Co worship night I attended has never left me. In that moment, I knew I had to reclaim that place.

It was too much like Eden to me. It holds me too tightly and finds me on just the right nights. There are too many moments when I'm carried up and away. There are too many memories full of love to let this place go because of one bad memory.

I didn't realize how close I was to doing that until Drew Holcomb and the Neighbors took the stage and took my breath away.

It's that balance I'm always trying to find, that line I'm working not to cross. It's the line between "There is nothing good in this place for you anymore, you should walk away" and the line that tells me to redefine the place and grow memories there again.

MY CHURCH SPLIT when I was a freshman in college, and my family left along with many others that year. It was strange for that to happen while I was away at the University of Georgia. The place I grew up attending would still have services every Sunday and take their students to camp every summer and serve Wednesday night supper in the Family Life Hall. It would all keep going. I just would never be back there. I lost that place in a way I could never have dreamed.

And we were church kids, you know? I used to say, "If the doors were unlocked and the Coke machine was taking quarters, I was there." There is no place, besides the home on Ebenezer Road, that holds more memories for me than that church building. So it wasn't that a Sunday morning tradition would change. It was that twenty years later, I can still drive by it, right in the middle of town, and look at any window and tell you what room that is and where it leads and what my experience was there.

Long after my family had left the church, I drove by and cut through the parking lot for some reason. I noticed the doors to the student area, where I had spent countless hours of my middle and high school years, were propped open. So I decided to trespass. I parked my car and walked into the VERY OPEN DOORS. (I did not even touch them and the statute of limitations on trespassing has long passed anyway.) I slowly crossed the threshold on this average Tuesday afternoon and expected an alarm to go off or a person to tell me to leave. But neither happened. So I just kept walking. I stuck my head into my eighth-grade Sunday school classroom, I walked into the bathroom where I had bullied someone and they never came back to church (I feel terrible about it), I passed the place beside the kitchen where some guys had been roughhousing and busted through the wall, I stepped into the room where we had small group for years.

And it didn't feel like anything. I had this moment. I remember it like it was yesterday, though it wasn't (again, statute of limitations). The visit felt empty and the building felt empty and it didn't give me any of the feels or full-heart moments that I expected. It was all empty.

Losing a place happens. It doesn't cost the memories. It just costs the hope of what could still be there.

BUT AS FOR the Ryman Auditorium, Drew was good and right and I didn't lose that place. He sang songs from his album "Dragons" and it's one of the best written and performed albums I've ever heard. The audience and I sang at the top of our lungs and I cried once. I looked around the room, sitting in a familiar section with a familiar view, and thanked God for places that hold more than just humans and pews. They hold memories and they hold space and they hold who we were, who we are, and what we love.

# The Pet Shop

I HAD A PUPPY for six days.

If you've listened to my podcast, particularly episodes in the spring of 2019, you know I have wanted a dog for a long time. Jenna and I were on a flight in January and I took two quizzes to see what kind of dog would work for me, and from that day forward, I was on a mission. I wanted a dog. To be exact, I wanted a cavapoo. The cavapoo, sometimes also called a Cavoodle, is a Cavalier King Charles Spaniel partnered with a Miniature Poodle. I WANTED A CAVOODLE.

I don't know what made me want a dog so much that year. Honestly, it just sounded like fun. A companion, a friend, something I could care for and something that I would be responsible for.

There's a weird thing that happens when you are unmarried in your late thirties and you have no children or pets. You realize that while your friends were being responsible to the children they were raising or the spouse they were sleeping with, you were just being you. And this isn't a grass is always greener story—these are just facts. As a single woman, my life has been relatively all about me. And while that can seem fun—well it is—at some point, I began to wonder if I was missing out on something because I wasn't having to sacrifice for anyone else. There just comes a point when you've done you for so long that you start to think maybe there is something to the joy others feel when they don't get sleep and when they are covered in poop but their lives still seem to be full and joyful.

I didn't know that experience, and it felt like I was missing out on fun and didn't even realize it. Maybe that sounds crazy, but there was a whisper question in my mind, wondering if there is something to searching for Eden in loving someone else more than you love yourself. I felt that desire growing in me, the desire to know what it could be like if I wasn't the most important living being in my own story.

Research proves it is true; pets make your life better. For people who live alone, a recent study found that owning a dog can decrease the risk of death by 33 percent and risk of cardiovascular death by 36 percent (compared to single folks without a pet).[1] Better for your life. Better for your heart.

And I could see it in my friends' lives. I could see how they loved their dogs, how they prioritized them, and how they also seemed to still have an active social life, which mattered to me.

The thought of it just started spinning in my mind. I'm a slow decision maker for big things like this, so I started talking about it and thinking about it in the winter, searching online and asking friends, stalking breeder litters and adoption sites and businesses, but I didn't find the right puppy for me until September.

But I knew when I saw her. Her name on the website was Sequoia, but she was tiny. A total oxymoron—such a little gal with such a big name. I thought I wanted a dude dog until I saw her. (For months everyone told me that I'd want a girl, not a boy. They were right after all.) She had already been matched with a family and for some reason that had fallen apart, so she was ready to be adopted.

I sent the email that I was interested and in a matter of hours, she was mine. She would be at my house in two weeks. I immediately called Dave's wife, Annie Barnes, and asked her kids what we should name her. Ben said Slushie. I laughed. Zanna said Helen. I laughed harder and I knew. Helen was her name. Helen F. Downs.

The next day was a Saturday, and I was watching football with some friends. I had two weeks to read books and prep my house and do all the things to get ready for a long, long, long-awaited puppy. But then my phone rang, and the caller told me it would not be two weeks. Helen would be at my house in twenty-four hours.

My palms started sweating, I got giddy, and I got in my car with two friends who were in from out of town. Betsy and Ashley and I rushed to the local puppy store, Nashville Pet Products Center. It is the store EVERY pet owner suggested to me. I acted like a rich person that afternoon—just pointing to everything that the woman said my puppy might possibly need and saying, "I'll take it!" Toys galore. A few bags of snacks. A teething ring (WAIT—PUPPIES LOSE THEIR TEETH? I did not know enough). A crate that I would call her palace. Can you just imagine a funnier thing than telling a puppy named Helen F. Downs to go to her Crate Palace? It just felt so right. I was suddenly very prepared.

Around 3:00 on Sunday afternoon the van pulled up and a kind older guy named Jack stepped out and slid open a door and there was Sequoia. There was Helen. She looked just like her pictures. My mini cavapoo, only two months old, was just barely the length of my forearm and weighed in at an estimated four pounds.

She was a glorified footlong sub sandwich covered in fur of every shade, from the patches of white over her eyes to her apricot sides down to her black tail. I was in love.

I hadn't lived with a pet in twenty years and I have never really loved my friends' pets, so I didn't know this feeling would be so complete in just a day. Just a moment. But honestly, it wasn't a moment. It was months of looking and hoping, hours of conversations with a variety of friends and mentors, prayers prayed, then suddenly she was here. I fell in love in a moment with a dog I had known for minutes but my heart had known for almost a year.

I teared up as she jiggled around in my arms and leapt from couch cushion to pillow to me to pillow. She had puppy energy, but they had also told me she was fun and energetic. It was part of how I knew she was the right dog for me. Her description said, "Full of fun but also a leader. Independent but loves to snuggle." Could I have found a more Annie dog?!? Helen was proving herself to be true to those descriptions in the first few minutes. I was laughing, and tearing up, and I knew my life had changed.

The day the emails were flying back and forth between her current owner and myself, I asked God if I was doing the right thing. To me (and also to you), He is that kind of God who will step into every situation with me and give me direction if I ask for it. I don't like making big decisions alone, so having God whisper into them, even about owning a puppy, is comforting to me.

I opened my daily devotional app and it read Exodus 23:20 (NIV) out loud to me. "See, I am sending an angel ahead of you to guard you along the way and to bring you to the place I have prepared."

A guard and a guide. That's what Helen would be for me, bringing me to a place that God had prepared for me. As she bounded from here to there to everywhere in my little living room, I saw her as that guard and guide. Since Helen was only footlong sub size, I wasn't going to depend on her to guard me from any large person or animal—I would probably be THAT kind of guard here in our little family—but I knew she was guarding me from something and guiding me to something.

Jack stayed for a bit and explained some things I didn't know, Helen peed on the rug, and then Jack was off and away in his van and I was entrusted with this little gal's life. She looked at me like she knew we were both in over our heads—me the most, but she seemed to sense she hadn't come into the home of a low-energy lady either.

The stats were true. My heart was healthier from moment one. Helen and I clicked right away. We both laughed (I don't know how to explain that I know that's true, but I do), we took a selfie, and I sat on the rug and held her. Before I called any friends, before I showed her to anyone, I wanted some moments of just us. I didn't want to be called a "dog mom." Helen has an actual dog mom who birthed her. I'm just her human. Her Annie.

The first day was a lot of learning and a lot of FaceTiming and a lot of fun. The second day she came to work with me, and Jenna loved her. She settled into her Crate Palace well, both at my house and at the office. I got home from work on Monday, and she still didn't smell like me. She smelled like wherever she had come from. So after dinner, I decided to give her a bath. I only had people shampoo and she hated every second of it and barely looked me in the eye when it was done, but we survived. And as we sat on the floor of the living room, playing with her lamb chop squishy toy and her stuffed squirrel, my face started to itch. Not a lot, not terribly, but it was a familiar feeling.

Because of that annoying dairy allergy, I'm familiar with the signs of an allergic reaction, and what was happening to my face with Helen is what happens to my face with milk.

But I couldn't be allergic to a cavapoo. They're hypoallergenic. So what was happening on day two? The first day was fine. I refused to believe I was allergic to Helen. She was my guard and my guide.

I spent the next three days on the phone with vets and human doctors and pet expert friends. My face continued to react, then so did my skin and eventually my lungs. I got my house cleaned and Helen had a sleepover party with a friend, just to see if maybe it was something in my house. I saw my naturopath and I shampooed Helen again, this time with dog shampoo. I did everything I could think to do, but the delayed hypersensitivity reaction continued and increased, and I wept my way through it.

Because I knew what my body was telling me.

I was allergic to this beautiful sable-colored gal, and my heart could not handle what I knew was coming next.

If there really is something powerful about falling in love, if this whole thing had been a search for the deeper thing I felt I had lost at some point, I was now about to lose it again. What does it all mean when the thing you love is the thing you lose, far before you thought you would?

On the Friday morning of that first week, just six days after Jack left her in my care, Helen and I loaded up in my RAV4 at 5:00 and headed across the state of Tennessee to hand her over to a foster family until she would be rehomed with a forever family.

I cried the whole drive. But that was nothing new; I'd been crying for days. When I pictured things in the future, like Christmas, I grieved. My mind's eye can see the whole story long before it's written, and I saw a long life with Helen. I grieved the loss of a companion and the loss of a friend. I grieved deeply the trust and bond we had built that she didn't know I was about to break. I cried, I talked to her, and I thanked her for some deeper moments in my heart that she had directly given me. I rolled down the window twice because my lungs felt so tight in her presence with us trapped in my little car that I couldn't breathe. The decision was right, everyone (including me) agreed with that, and my lungs confirmed it. But it didn't help and wasn't healing my broken heart.

Helen and I had been together practically constantly. When she yelped in her Crate Palace, she was yelping for me. When she looked around the corner from the kitchen to the living room, she was looking for me. When we walked outside to go potty in the middle of the night, multiple times a night every night, it was just us. My guard and my guide and me.

Pastor Kevin, the lead pastor at my church and known to the *That Sounds Fun* podcast listeners as "pastor of the pod," came to the office the day before Helen left me. He held her and she fell asleep almost instantly. (Another proof that she was my kind of gal—we can fall asleep anywhere.) And he prayed. He prayed for her, for me, for my health, and for our hearts. He looked into my eyes as the tears poured down my cheeks, and he said, "I think this is a test from God. Not for Him to see if you would pass, but for you to see if you could." I looked at him and listened as he continued. "Maybe you needed to know that you could love this much. Maybe you needed to see that you would be willing to sacrifice time and money and sleep for someone else that you loved more than yourself."

He was right. Maybe Helen guided me to a place where I could learn that I could love. Not learn to love but learn that it is already in me. Maybe she guarded me from a life where I thought I didn't have what it takes to parent, to love a man day in and day out and serve him well, to sacrifice for a human baby. Helen didn't tell me I could do it, she told me I already had. Maybe Helen came into my life to remind me that my heart was still beating and had everything it needed to love deeper than I thought I could.

I am an amateur at this. It sounded so fun to have a companion, to have someone who depended on me, to have someone waiting for me when I got home from the office or a trip or a date. I didn't want her to leave, and I told her that in the car as the sun rose in front of us and we got closer and closer to the meet-up spot.

Matt, the foster dad who met me at the BP gas station off the interstate, arrived soon after I did. Helen played in the grass as I cried. And as I moved her Crate Palace into Matt's car, I kept holding her and saying thank you. And ten minutes later, after stories were told and tears were cried and reassurances (from Matt to me) were made, we both drove away. Me heading back to Nashville alone, Matt back to his home and his family with my girl Helen.

THERE IS EDEN even in loss. There is deep joy in profound connectedness, even if it doesn't last. I am heartbroken and in love and I will never forget Helen.

I gave Matt all the toys and snacks and accoutrements I bought for Helen. Except one. That Saturday we had gone to the pet store, the day before Helen arrived at Harvest House and in my life two weeks premature, my friend Betsy stood behind me as I searched for the right collar and leash. She tapped me on the shoulder and in her hands was a chew toy that was shaped like a Coke Icee, my all-time favorite drink. I laughed, but it was also a sign to me. A reminder that, yes, God was in this. And I bought that Coke Icee chew toy. And when I loaded all of Helen's things into my car to eventually transfer them into Matt's car, I left the Coke Icee toy on my dining room table. It remains a reminder to me of the week, of Helen, and of the ways that searching for Eden can matter, even when it hurts.

# Sevier Park

I LOOKED DOWN at my new tattoo as I drove home from dropping Helen off with Matt. "Savor this." I had really done it to myself this time, tattoo-wise, because I didn't want to savor this AT ALL. I didn't want to feel this anymore and I didn't want to think about what all this means and I was just sad and had just about no time to actually grieve what I lost.

I preached at church the Sunday after Helen left. It was strange. It was like she was never here but was also just a thought away. She was quickly adopted by another family and given a different name in a different state, which is probably better for me.

Pastor Drew, the creative pastor at our church, brought his two youngest kids with him to church that day: AJ and Bentley. His wife, Jamie, and their two oldest, Grace and Emory, were out of town that week. All four of the kids call me Aunt Annie, and I love it so much. I have a few nicknames with a few different families. Aunt Annie is a good one. Two families call me AnnieDowns, like one name, since there are already a few Annies in our kids' lives. But I think my favorite nickname is Crazy Annie. It's the best nonfamily "aunt" kind of name that anyone could think of for me. The kids yell it across the street, across the playground, across the kitchen. It's the only thing they know me as. (Because yes, I am for sure the silliest, craziest adult they know. And I'm glad for it.)

But Pastor Drew's kids stick with Aunt Annie. After I finished preaching the sermon in the first service of the day, AJ said I needed a haircut and that I coughed too much. (That's real family talk and that cough was definitely Helen's fault. Allergies, man!) The kids and I sat together between services that day. Me with my new inhaler (also thanks to Helen) and Bentley—Drew's five-year-old daughter—with her sequined cat-ear headband. We laughed as she sat in my lap and ate a Rice Krispie Treat. She hates taking selfies. I absolutely love them and love to beg her and snap pictures until she says no or says "PLEASE DON'T POST THAT." (And I don't.)

I got home Sunday night and was scrolling through pictures from the day, and I saw a hilarious one of Bentley and me. She's wrapped in my arms, her head laid right into the nook of my elbow. She's half smiling at the camera, her little sequined cat ears glimmering under the fluorescent lights of the church. I texted it to her parents, and I was typing before I was thinking and I said, "Who needs a dog when I already have a cat?" It was a joke (obviously), but it also spoke to something deeper in me—something I didn't quite know how to put words around until that moment with Bentley.

I DIDN'T KNOW what it would be like for my best friends to have kids. They are little joys who I like to call my MiniBFFs.

I didn't know what it would be like to love the kids of my friends. But it is the most fun.

It started with Jarrett. He was born while I was still teaching elementary school, and I called in for a substitute teacher to cover my class so I could be at the hospital when he was born. And it's been me and him (and his parents, of course) for the last thirteen years. He was two when I moved to Nashville, and I think he was the hardest person for me to leave behind. I came home for Christmas that first year after I had moved away, and as soon as I walked in the door, he screamed my name and stood up from the chair in the dining room, ran across the living room, jumped on the couch on the way, ran the length of the couch to the front door, and bounded into my arms. It still makes me tear up to tell you about it. It was such a significant moment for me. And after Jarrett, my friends just. kept. having. kids. It has been the absolute most fun.

We get this choice as single people surrounded by peers who have become parents. We can either make new friends with new adults or make friends with the children of our old friends. Those are the options. And for my married friends, you can either let your single friends be friends with your kids or, honestly, you will probably lose them. Sometimes that is fine. I totally get it.

But it feels like maybe we are doing family wrong here in Western society anyway. Shouldn't everyone feel like they fit somewhere? It doesn't have to be your nuclear family—none of mine live in this town where I live—because any family system can welcome you and include you.

In one of my all-time favorite romantic comedies, *While You Were Sleeping*, the main character, Lucy, is talking with her boss about family systems. He says, "Lucy, you are born into families, you do not join them like you do the Marines."[1] But I'm just not sure that's true. I think family is so much more than the definition we give it. I'm not talking about *framily*, some weird word people have made up for friends who are like family. I'm talking about actual family.

ONE NIGHT I was over at Dave and Annie Barnes's house, a stop I make on a lot of evenings after work. The three kids were running around like crazy: Sam looking for a snack, Zanna taking dolls and puzzles in and out of the playroom, and Ben kicking and dribbling the soccer ball up and down the hallway. Annie and I sat around the table as I filled out paperwork for Onsite. I needed to put an emergency contact on the form, and I looked up at her and thought for a minute. "Annie, will you be my emergency contact?" She smiled and said of course. And it led us to a conversation about what it looks like to really be committed like that, to choose family, even if you aren't related. We talked about the actual word and the actual commitment and it changed things for us.

I've spent a lot of evenings at the Barnes's house, but that one was super special. To be loved like that, invited in like that, spoken to about commitment like that. It warmed my heart. And the kids kept running around and Ben kept asking me to play and Zanna started crying and life went on right around the moment I joined their family.

I WAS RECENTLY transporting a whole bunch of boxes full of books from the office down to my car. I loaded them onto a rolling chair, stacked three boxes too high, and rolled onto the elevator. As I went to exit the elevator at the ground floor, one of the wheels caught on the slit where the door opens. The top two boxes immediately made moves like they were the Red Sea parting and I knew I couldn't save the one on the right, but I thought I might be able to save the one on the left. So as it tumbled I stuck my arm out to catch the box. Instead of landing in my arms, the edge of the box of books slammed into my forearm and then fell to the ground. But it hit RIGHT on my "savor this" tattoo.

The pain of that moment felt so profoundly true. I have chosen to love deep and wide in this time of my life, and while I'm trying to stay in it and feel it, it is bruising me too. It is hurting me right in the place where I'm trying to savor it all. Where I'm trying to really be in the moment and live what is right in front of me.

And guess what? This is what happens when you love. This is what happens when I love. There is no protecting your savor this from bruises if you're going to love and live your life.

I'm scared to be brave today, too, if that helps you at all. I'm scared to love today, scared to hope. I'm worried that I'm going to look like a fool or end up more bruised. And if I'm being totally honest with you, every time I get a bruise, I want to become the girl in the plastic bubble and not let anyone near my heart. But I think that's what my MiniBFFs do for me. They keep me soft. They bump into the bruises but don't hurt them.

I PARKED MY car across the street and walked down to Sevier Park. It's the park in the middle of our neighborhood, and all the kids ride bikes there and play on the playground. On Tuesdays in particular, when the 12th South Farmers Market is going, we tend to find ourselves heading there at the end of the work and school day, my friends and their kids and me. One day I watched as my MiniBFF Theo biked toward me. As he got closer, I worried he was going too fast and would fall and get hurt. I wanted to yell out, but then I saw that his parents were super calm and trusting. If they weren't worried, I wasn't going to worry. Theo's face was pure excitement as he careened toward me. That kid was having the best time. I feel like I learned a lesson that day at Sevier Park. I learned that fun is worth the risk. Honestly, it's all worth the risk.

I HAD A MASSIVE friendship misunderstanding recently and I don't know how to fix it. I want to, I think, but I don't even know the first move when I only heard about this problem secondhand. As soon as I heard about the issue, I drove to the Barnes's house. Annie and our friend from across the street, Amy, were both sitting on the front porch, ready to go on a walk. I got out of the car and walked up and burst into tears. That's love, isn't it? Having a place where you can melt down and break down and laugh and play soccer and just show up when you need a hug.

There's something Eden-like about that, even in the sadness. I don't think it was ever sad there before Adam and Eve sinned, but there is something about having a place to come home to that feels like the thing we can't find.

I work so hard in my life to feel at home on my own. And it comes so, so close to being enough, but it just isn't. I don't want to admit that. I want you to think I'm fine alone and

I don't need people. This is where we've broken Western culture—by hearing and repeating the lie that alone is strong and together is weak. That we should all be capable of living absolutely independent of each other. To need others is to be weak or unable to do life well. If you do it alone, SUCCESS. Look at you. You don't need anyone. Congrats.

But it's just not true. It lacks the center thing—it lacks love. Isolation doesn't lead to flourishing; isolation leads to death. What we need is love.

I OPENED MY PHONE the other day to see that my friend had sent a video from her family with two of my MiniBFFs. In the video, the little girl says, "AnnieDowns, AnnieDowns?" and her older brother says, "AnnieDowns, I love you. Look at this" before throwing something across the room that the mom doesn't get on video. I so love being loved by these kids. It changes me for the better every day.

I have always dreamed of being a mom. I wasn't one of those little girls who played house and said I wanted to be a mommy when I grew up, but deep in me, I knew I always really, really loved children and wanted to have my own. And yet here I am, decades down the road, and I don't. I do not know what it looks like to have small people with some of my features. I don't know what it's like to look at baby pictures of my parents and see the same eyes in a new baby I am holding. I don't know anything about being an actual person's parent. And I'm grieved by it at times.

But I know the feeling of love. And I trust my gut enough to know it when I feel it. Ephesians 3:20 is so deeply true. This love for, and from, my MiniBFFs is a love that is more than I could have asked for or imagined. It's not a parent love, but it's not a friend love either. And it's not a nanny or babysitter love because I don't do that anymore—it takes a tougher and more rested person than me to nanny, that is for sure. It's this other thing, this Eden thing, this powerful exchange between a trusting child and a trustworthy adult and trusting parents. It lights me up because it feels like God saw a gaping hole in my heart and filled it to overflowing with a collection of children that I couldn't have birthed, even on my best day. It's this other kind of love that says God sees me and hears me. It says that my prayers have been answered, even if the kids don't have my parents' eyes. It is the kind of love that tells me to keep choosing hope, because there is a gift in the choosing, a gift that exceeds all expectations.

As I'm typing on a Wednesday night, a sad Wednesday that didn't quite go as planned, where having family would have been helpful for me, I got this text from Amber.

> Tonight when Matt asked the kids who they wanted to pray for, Aury's first response was "AnnieDowns" and then they all prayed for you. That was the majority of the prayer.

It makes me cry just sitting here typing about it. It's a kind of love I didn't know to ask for, a love that is so profound and deep and other, it just must be a gift.

Catching chickens with my husband SHERISE | Adventures with my husband JEANNETTE | Traveling with my FRIENDS NICHOLE | Bangin' on my tambourine BRITTANY | Front porch rocking with family JENNI | All the books. No people. REBEKAH | Drinking coffee on my porch ASHLEY | Bath, coffee, friends, Banff, road trip ALLISON | Coffee and laughter with friends CINDY | Laughing and eating with friends SARAH | Riding a beach cruiser with friends AUDREY | My girls, Libby and Harper LAURA | A break in the clouds BETH | Sipping coffee and reading AUBREY | Nature meditation in the Olympics STACY | Building memories with my people ALYSSA | Alaskan cruise with my hubby MEGAN | A massage on Cozumel Beach KATY | Playing board games with friends MARIAH | Enjoying my awesome NYC DENISE | Hiking in every national park SARAH | Rainy day painting with coffee LIZ | Beach, coffee + Young Life camp KAYLA | Week-long best friend vacation ALICIA | Kayaking with friends MICHELLE | Sewing, crocheting, Cricuting, making gifts CADY | Hammock, good book, chai latte JEN | Attending a sports event KIMBERLY | Showing Morgan horses with family CELIA | Beach/lake with my people AMANDA | Learning something new MIKE | Baking all the yummy things KARYN | Leading Fremont Young Life ZACH | Christmas movies and hot chocolate KATHLEEN | Holding miracle baby in my arms LEAH | Assuring people they're not forgotten AMY | Outdoors. Good Books. Coffee. Friends. JD | Playing guitar at a lake OLIVIA | Riding dragons BEATTIE | Cozy blankets, musicals, wine, Gospel-Enneq-talks TAYLER | Loving those around me well ASHLEE | Watching Marvel movies ALBERTO | Mountain hiking with my husband LAUREN | First kiss as a married couple CALLYSSA | Time with my family STEPHANIE | Drinking coffee with friends CHRISTINA | Toes in the sand TIERRA | Get a massage SARAH | Going to an *NSYNC concert LIZ | Book club with my people LAURA | Arm-knitting scarves MJ | Laughing until breathless with family ANGEL | An unknown adventure with girlfriends LAURA | Travel the world with framily DARETH | Relaxing at the lake JESSA | Shopping at consignment stores SARAH | Movie and dinner with hubs SYLVIA | Taking kiddos to the zoo KALLAE | Traveling to somewhere new KAYLAH | Hiking with my family BETHANNE | Restoring a vintage camper SHELLY | Glitter party KIMBERLEE | Walking in Norman with Will ALI | Become fluent in ASL BRITTANY | A pilgrimage around the world KYLIE | Buying new socks MELODY | Girls' trip with AudreyClaire CONNIE | Playing board games with friends EMILY | A home filled with DIY ABBY | Doing life with best friends RUTH | Hugging my best friend's kids MEGHAN | Exploring new cities with Micah CASEY | Traveling lesser-known countries KATRINA | Road trip around Ireland MANDY | Vacationing on a houseboat ARNETA | Our anniversary trip to Israel EMILY | Brunch on the beach RACHEL | Vacation with my husband CLAIR | Jamming out at a concert JENNIFER | A weekend in Lake Tahoe TATE | Reading by a fireplace KIRSTIN | Baking Christmas cookies ANNA | A wandering stroll through London CAROLINE | Exploring more of God's creation SAM | Friends, family, food, fresh air MEG | Long walks in the woods JILL | Traveling the world with friends ASHLEY | Creating something new JORDANNA | Sunrise over the Chesapeake ALLISON | Swimming in a mountain pool BARBARA | Camping, beaches, books, and babies MICHELLE | Being with my Gal Pals MELANIE | Going home to my dog LOUISA | Axe throwing SARAH | Loving Jesus and Target MACKENZIE | Playing with a golden retriever JENNA | Spending time with my family STEPHANIE | Family, football, food, faith, frequently AMY | Graduating won't He do it? CAITLYN | Traveling to new places AMANDA | Time with my favorite people STACY | Laughing with my family BARBARA | Manicure then hiking CAITLIN | Time with my adult children LESLIE | Beach day and a book LINDSAY | Hot-air balloon festivals ELLEN | Seashell hunting at the beach CASSIE | New restaurants and meaningful conversation KIRSTEN | Game night with my people LYDIA | Vacation in Ireland CARRIE | Showing our son the world KATARINA | Hiking with my friends STEPHANIE | A trip to Lake Superior ALLYSON | Couch cuddles with my puppies HANNAH | Time with my little friends TATUM | Hiking with my husband BRITTANY | A day of giving JENNIFER | A spa day LINDSEY | Trying something new AMY | Cabin weekend with friends KAYLA | Taking a nap without alarm DANIELLE | Sleepover weekend with my nephews JENN | Jam on guitar, sing w/daughter ANDREW | Weekend trips with my husband DAWN | Sipping a delicious chai latte JENNY | Going to Europe with Chase COURTNEY | Creating space to be real JULIE | Board games with my husband SUNHAE | National park hiking with husband JILL | Traveling with my family KAREN | Spending time with family MANDILYNN | Reading in my bed KODEE | Making food with my people CATE | Celebrating everything, Enneagram 7 style KATIE | Vacation and books with friends AMY | Knitting while watching Hallmark movies JESSICA | First date in Atlanta TAYLOR | Traveling across country with family STACI | Seeing shows in the West End of London JENNY | Taking a trip with friends LINDSAY | Drinking good coffee with friends DARBI | Cheering on the Georgia Bulldawgs KRISTY | Decorating for Christmas MELISSA | Watching Hallmark movies with Elizabeth MELANIE | Wandering new city with husband KACI | Playing Tennis with my ALTAteam JOY |

A mother/daughter cruise MADDIE | Quitting my desk job DIANA | Baking with my mom SOPHIE | Backpacking through Europe with friends EMILY | Family book read-alouds TAMMI | Kitchen dance parties ANNETTE | Intentional, authentic conversations SHANTEL | Sunrise hike on the Blueridge KATE | Kayaking in West Virginia ROBIN | Beaching ALL DAY CATHERINE | Stargazing in Westcliffe, Colorado ALLIE | Cocoa & conversation with friends DEBORAH | Heaven LYNDSI | Front porch, hot coffee, heart friend SARA | Snuggling my babies CALLIE JO | A 410 Bridge mission trip ERIN | Walking with my dogs and husband KIERSTEN | Kid-free hammock lounging while reading MEGAN | Spending time with God MARY | Giving genuine compliments to people JENNIFER | Visiting NYC at Christmastime MEGHAN | Going on another cruise vacation SARAH | Cross-stitching, petting my dog RACHAEL | Traveling somewhere new with my husband MARIA | Exploring new breweries with friends MEGHAN | Hiking national parks with family KAREN | Loving on my littles KAYLA | Going to concerts with friends MADI | Walks on the beach ANNELI | Singing in the car CAROLYN | Watching *I Love Lucy* reruns HANNAH | Window shopping with my bestie SARAH | Gator football games with friends CAROLINE | Road trip from Canada to Atlanta SARAH-JANE | Campfire + mountains + friends JENNY | Reading on the beach EMILY | Belly laughing with my family ABBIE | Getting cozy with a book MEGAN | A day with my family ANNIE | South America trip with Teresa LAUREN | Coffee and fellowship with BFFs TRISHA | The *That Sounds Fun* podcast ROB | Running on the beach LINDSEY | Touring the Glen Canyon Dam BRITTANY | Long runs with good friends JENNIFER | My toes in white sand AMY | Being with my MiniBFFs ALYSHIA | Starbucks Mondays with my mom LIZ | Eat my way around Disney KELLY | Reading in bed with chocolate MARY | Cozy blanket, tea, reading outside ASHLEY | Cheering for the GA Bulldawgs ROBYN | Skiing. Peppermint cone at Disneyland. KRISTEN | Audible listening while jigsaw puzzling AMANDA | Seeing Iy/o meet Mickey Mouse LAURA | Beach, coffee, book :) CANDY | Hiking with friends JANELLE | Spending time with amazing girlfriends MEGAN | Doing something/going somewhere new ABBY | Going to South Africa PAIGE | A good iced chai latte SOPHIE | Me and my man traveling KIM | Dance party in the living room TARA | Game night with friends SHANNON | Living on mission with friends LAUREN | Being with my people AMANDA | Having tea with Queen Latifah ALLIE | Outdoor adventures with my people LAUREN | Hugging kitties, teaching, knitting hats BETH | Water aerobics with pumpkins LORI | Home after a long year JILL | Backpack hiking MALLORY | Sewing with my grammy BRITTANY | Marrying my best friend JENNIFER | Coffee dates with intentional conversations BROOKE | Laughter, coffee, camp friends SARAH | Black Friday shopping every year CHELSEA | A last-minute beach vacation AMANDA | Listening to podcasts and books DAMARIS | Stargazing with my husband DAI | Ballroom dancing with my husband JULIA | Having a classic movies marathon SARAH | Rearranging furniture KAITLYN | Relaxing by the Caribbean Sea TIFFANY | Dinner with my whole family ALEXANDRA | Discovering a new favorite book KATE | Morning Bible study with coffee JENA | Running KAITLYN | Reading on the beach JESS | A quiet day to crochet SHEENA | Coffee + friends + chick flick JAMESON | Traveling to experience new cultures HEIDI | Backpacking Europe with my friends MADISON | Vacation to Italy SAMANTHA | Walking in nature DANIELLE | Couch, Baking, family, and being outside KC | Gathering together for family dinner HEATHER | Snuggling with my two dogs SARAH | Europe with people I love CATHERINE | Monthly hike coffee, PJs, and movies RACHAEL | Cooking and listening to podcasts ALYSSA | Family beach time warm weather TAMI | Going on a family cruise MELISSA | Making pottery with my friends with my bestie MARSHA | Losing seventy-five pounds in 2019 NEELI | Hugging a cheetah KRISTEN | Coaching basketball with Jac MAURA | Making barefoot in my kitchen STOREY | Counseling, mentoring, and momming SHIANN | Creating objects in clay KIM | Worshiping and singing with my husband MADI | Getting married ALYSSA | BFFs all-inclusive AMALIE | Sunny beaches in Mexico LAURA | Attending Evensong at Westminster Abbey AMY | Hiking in snowy mountains MADI | Going to a musical JULIE | Skydiving from 14,000 feet up PAM | resort adventure LAURA | Winning a mad game of ERS ASHER | Sitting on a San Diego beach MELINDA | Family reunion vacation JACLYNNE | Trail runs in the woods ABBY | A good used bookstore KRIS | Dancing slurpees with my people RUTHIE | Going to the beach EMMA | Stopping to admire the view LIZ | Belting musicals in ocean waves KIM | Hanging out with Yanna TAMARRAH | College roommate reunion weekend BECKA | Making Micah (son, 10 months) giggle MELANIE | A book on a beach BRITTANEE | Kissing my sweet babies ALEXIS |

Reading an entire book on a Saturday ERICA | Laughing, sitting on the beach AMY | Alaskan cruise with my family GENEVA | Sipping on lattes with friends MERCEDES | Being with my YOKE kids SARAH | GROWING in who I am CASSY | Discovering a new, fun workout CASSANDRA | Christmas trip to NYC AMY | Reading by the fire PEYTON | Exploring the Canadian Rockie Mountains CARLYSLE | Working puzzle with family TERRI | Reading with coffee + a blanket NOWELLE | Starting a family SAMANTHA | Campfire and s'mores with friends MADDI | Playing soccer in the rain MICHAELA | Hiking in New Zealand ALISHA | Time with family in God's creation ASHLEY | Alone with books and coffee BRITTANY | Understanding people and their emotions TIFFANY | Making breakfast with my roommates SOPHIA | Climbing a mountain with friends MELANIE | Traveling the world with friends ELISA | Friends, food, firelight, insane laughter LAURA | Sharing Jesus with the unreached KARA | Curling up with a book NEIL | Having a party every day MADISON | Having Cafecito in Costa Rica SARAH | Favorite coffee shop with friends KELLY | Morning walks to Frothy Monkey ALISON | Travel the world JESSICA | River skiing with my family LAURIE | Being outside; time with family LORIE | Disneyland Tokyo with my favorites SARAH | Taking a midday nap BLAIR | Helicopter ride over Niagara Falls JENNA | Spending time with my family MAELYN | Game night with Mom Friends JAIMIE | Watching Christmas movies with Mom ELLIE | Tea and conversation with friends MARISSA | Kayaking on the bay ASHLEY | Visit NYC at Christmas SUSAN | A movie and hot cocoa COURTNEY | Family time, coffee drinking, crocheting KENDRA | Skiing with my son HOLLY | Going to the beach MOLLY | Sanford Stadium on fall Saturdays KATE | A Friday off of work JENNY | Best friends playing games together XUAN | Exploring our national parks KATHERINE | Traveling, drinking coffee, tasting EVERYTHING KATE | Reading. Family. Friends. Teaching. Dancing. MONICA | Busch Gardens with my husband MEGHAN | National parks with friends RYAN | Spending time with my son TRACY | Singing "Wonderwall" at Allianz Field VICKI | Going on a tropical vacation SIERRA | Kayaking on the Susquehanna River JIM | Hope reunions with my besties SARAH | Strolling through Epcot CARSON | Hallmark Christmas movie marathon KRISTIN | Girls' trip to the mountains GINA | Making dinner in a wood fireplace EMORY | Surprising kids with Disney trip KATIE | Family game night TUMOM | Experiencing nature in every season SHANNON | Going shopping with my daughter SUSAN | Reading a good book NATALIE | Flying to attend a concert TRINA | Disney World with my people STEPHANIE | Exploring my new home—Korea RACHEL | A Stranger Things-themed party CHARISSA | Hike to a waterfall in Uganda ADRIENNE | Graduating from journalism school MIRANDA | Lattes. Mountain climbing. Movies. Snuggling. MOLLY | Friday night football KIM | Nature adventures with my son SHELLEY | Hiking to see Northern Lights KAITLYN | A concert with my husband ANGIE | Taking a pottery wheel class ALISON | I don't know. #Enneagram9 JENNYLYNN | Snorkeling in Cozumel RACHEL | World travel HEATHER | Making handmade ugly Christmas sweaters ALYSSABETH | Traveling around the world LAUREN | BELTING songs in the car TOWNSEND | Laughing hard with trusted friends KATHARINE | Snow day and hot cocoa ALISSA | Farmer's market strolls on Saturdays SAM | Puzzle parties REBEKAH | Eating Texas nights with friends JILL | Christmas movies, wine, and fireplaces RACHEL | Exploring all the national parks MAIRIN | Balcony reading with my corgi HEATHER | Vacation with my tacos with my hubs BRITTNEY | Kayaking,

miniBFFs BRENDA | Hanging with my best
Cozily watching Hallmark Christmas
Family mountain vacation. Also pizza.
the fireplace EMMA | Laughing at
Playing worship music with others
in the cold JENNY | Hot coffee and
Vacation, adventuring, new sites &
friends NIKKI | Camping in our
the car CHANELL | Eating disorder
and yoga CORRIN | Laughing &

people :) KIWI | Bike rides in the country TAYLOR | Smiles with our baby girl ELIZABETH | Tour of Italy with Joe DOREEN |
movies MADELEINE | Hiking somewhere I've never been FAWN | Bike rides in the country TAYLOR | My front porch GEREE |
solitude with God EMILY | Italy, wine, bread, my love RACHEL | Driving convertible in the rain RACHEL | Reading by

ARDEN | Coffee & a good book KELSEE | Savannah food & wine girls' weekend NATALIE | Reading by
stories with friends KAYLEE | Hiking a mountain with friends MIRANDA | Lake Day with my family EMILY |
LARISSA | Watching my kids perform MOLLIE | Kissing giraffes at Giraffe Manor EMILY | Hot chocolate
crochet ELISABETH | International food, history, and fun COLLEEN | Beach trip with friends APRIL |
experiences RACHEL | Petting cats & drinking coffee ANNABROOKE | Playing ultimate frisbee with
pop-up JENNIFER | Riding scooters downtown LINDSEY | Coffee with my people KAYLA | Singing in
recovery taco celebration TAYLOR | Hiking a 14'er in Colorado MADISON | Baking, embroidery,
singing KATHI | Travel with my boys TRICIA | Day off with my little SUE | Writing a book LAUREN |

Beaching at an all-inclusive resort NAN | Spending time investing in myself KALYN | Hammocking deep in the forest QUINN | Sharing charcuterie with friends ROSSIE | Hallmark movies and coffee ANDREA | Snuggly blanket by a fire LIBBY | Listening to Dolly running Codes Cove LAUREN | Adventures with my family NORA | Sitting on a Caribbean beach DIANE | Back porch coffee date ERIN | Drinking a perfectly crafted coffee ALVNA | Toddler dance parties DANIELLE | Cheering for Nashville Soccer Club SHELBY | European Disney Cruise REBEKAH | Visiting Nashville with my family OLIVIA | Cheering on UGA from Houston LAUREN | Loving God & loving people REBEKAH | Going for a drive KENZIE | War Eagling in Jordan Hare LAUREN | Box seat at the Tivoli TAYLOR | Beach trip with my husband REBECCA | Developing recipes people crave ALLY | Flight, beach, Hailey, Lily & Grace SARAH | Watching Netflix and reading LAUREN | Exploring a new place HANNAH | Training in taekwondo HOLLY | Eating snacks with my pals MEGAN | A hot-air balloon ride PEYTON | Good coffee with good friends KRISTA | Golfing on a summer evening MADELINE | A wedding with wildflowers 2020 KAYTLYN | Traveling with my husband HOLLY | A vacation with my husband JESS | Quiet mountain vacation BETHANY | Eating pasta in Italy ANDREA | Weekend getaway with my sisters RUTH | Anything and everything Christmas LIZ | Friends, family, travel, Enneagram, games TRICIA | New restaurants with old friends JYLLEA | REAGAN | Rope swinging into an M&M pit AMELIA | Spending time with my family AMY | Hugging grandchildren on my lap CYNDI | A weeklong birthday party JYLLEA | Weekend shopping with childhood friends KIMBERLEE | Dancing in the kitchen w/hubby OLIVIA | All fifteen grandkids at Disney DAWNA | Family sleepover by Christmas tree ELIZABETH | Having adventures in God's Creation KATIE | Sunshine time GRACE | Fast motorcycles on curvy roads FARAN | Coffee shop date with John JESSI | Hume Lake, California, hammock reading KATIE | Jesus telling me a joke CYNDI | Becoming the person God made MICHELE | Hiking day with my husband AMANDA | Shooting silly family videos MARIO | Taking a family cruise BETHANY | Girlfriends plus wine and cheese ELISE | Creating art/crafting all day CORRIE | Taking a life-changing risk HAYLEY | Thrift store shopping KATIEJO | Making music with friends ANNA | Flying to meet new niece HOLLI | Making love with my husband KIM | College family annual retreat KATHRYN | Working for the gathering place SYDNEY | Hosting a Christmas tea party STEPHANIE | Seeing Broadway musicals with friends BRANDI | Floating in the lake JUDI | Exploring the world COURTNEY | Finishing up grad school JEN | Going down a waterslide CASSIE | Binge watching my favorite show TRICIA | Climbing Mount Kilimanjaro CAROLYN | Good coffee with friends MORGAN | Reread Jane Austen's catalog MEGAN | Photographing colorful people and places KATHRYN | Family time at the beach MICAH | Dancing, reading, movies, laughing, eating CELESTE | Decorating for Christmas CAELEIGH | Become work-at-home Mama LAUREN | Traveling around Europe with friends LINDSEY | Hiking up a mountain ANNA-MARIE | Snowboarding on fresh powder MARY | Experiencing new places with loved ones ELESHIA | Walking and talking with Kam NAN | Coffee and a good book LISA | Snowboard all mountains in US SHANNON | Hearst Castle with my husband LAURA | Going to Scotland again AMY | Carousel ride with my grandpa BRI | Pizza. Sunshine. Coffee. Family. Naps. JESSIE | Night scootering with my buddies SANDHYA | Coffee and a good book JOHANNA | NALA | Lake Michigan with my kiddos LINDSAY | Watching classic musical movies SARAH | Hiking Devil's Tower with family CINDY | With family at lake cabin JOHANNA | Visiting all the national parks ANNA | Bubble bath, candles, and wine JULIE | Riding a llama LISSE | Quality time with family/friends TERI | Celebrating Christmas with family CHELSEA | Reading, hiking, horses, friends, family ALI | Cooking a meal for friends KATE | Lake day with my family ZACH | Hammocking across Spearfish Creek KAITLIN | Weekend road trips to Austin ERIN | Grabbing coffee with friends KRISTINA | Creating while drinking coffee KRISTINA | Beach. Book. Drink. JANET | Reading at the beach JODI | Buying red lipstick NATALIE | Heaven with my people ANNA | Cooking a meal for friends KATE | Sunny beach relaxation with family MEREDITH | Road trip with my love TINA | Celebrating life through new experiences SYDNEY | Hiking the Columbia Gorge NICOLE | Spending time with my niece BRITTANY | All my people laughing together KRISTI | Reading on my back porch BAILEY | Beach, waves, book, sweat, nap KRISTA | Disneyland with my family KATE | A Hawaiian vacation with husband APRIL | Visit all the national parks FELICIA | Late-night chats with pals HEATHER | Marvel movies with family ABIGAIL | Friends, charcuterie, and Christmas movies KAREN | Brett Eldredge's Ryman Christmas concert GRETCHEN | FaceTiming with my niece, Isla JACKIE | Charcuterie and wine with friends EMILIE | Ice skating to *NSYNC KOHLIE | Spending time with FUGE friends ABBY | Dancing with my man and kids DRE | A BIG ole dance party HEATHER | Tuesday coffee dates with bestie SEASON | Take a much-needed sabbath KATHLEEN | Ice skating on frozen bay BETSY | An art-filled Saturday MELISSA | Coffee. Blanket. Couch. Book. KELLEY BETH | Going to Disney World MARISSA | Baking the best cookies LIZ | Coffee, board games, and family JULIA | Taking a spin-cycling class CAITLIN | Swimming in clear blue water JULIE |

# Why You Need *a* Hobby

# Neighbors Restaurant

A WHILE BACK, my friend Laura and I met after work to catch up. Neighbors is a restaurant just over the Jefferson Street Bridge from Cross Point Church. My office used to be at the church and she lives in the same neighborhood, so it was an easy choice. She beat me there. She always does. And I came in with a gust of wind at my back and papers flying everywhere (or at least that's how it felt).

My days, in general, feel too rushed. I don't know why, and I don't really like it. Most days I am hopping from this place to that place, from this project to that project, out of one meeting and into another. It's usually the last meeting of the day when I really feel that windblown experience of my rushing in and sitting down and apologizing and laughing. Laura is used to this and to me. She's a business owner as well, so her schedule is packed from start to finish each day.

She had already ordered a gin and tonic. I ordered a cider. It's my favorite happy hour drink, especially when I am rushed and it's the summer and I just want to relax with a friend.

We quickly started chatting and catching up. She runs a magazine I love called *Good Grit*, and we have fun talking about business—the best days and the worst days, the ups and the downs. We also talked about relationships with men (me in dating, her in marriage to a man and parenting young men), our shared love of Onsite, and the way we saw God moving in our lives and the lives of the people we love.

We spun through all of those topics at Neighbors. I tend to find that even on the busiest days, just to sit and process through it all with someone slows down my mind and my heart. We talked about two friends who were struggling, whose lives seemed to be falling apart, and what we could do. There's never a good enough answer for how to help a broken story, and we talked about that too. And then, a little out of nowhere, Laura said, "I'm going to make a list of all the things I want to try."

And everything she listed required her to be an amateur. Everything she listed required her to fall in love in one way or another. Everything she listed was an activity that someone else would call a hobby.

LAURA WANTED TO MAKE a list because she needs space in her life and new experiences and I think, deep down inside, she needs to feed the hunger. "I think we are living in the hungriest generation ever," she told me. And I knew she wasn't just talking about food; she was talking about our souls. We fill our calendars and fill our lives and try to fill our bank accounts and our hearts, but what was it about that hunger for satisfaction that made her want to make a list? What about that list feels like a map to Eden?

Laura thought she needed a hobby or two. I would actually say we all do.

Hobbies make space. They remind us of something beautiful, and that good can come from nothing. That seeds become flowers and ingredients become soup and yarn becomes mittens. And when the whole world is broken, it's just nice to know we have the tiniest ability to put pieces together.

I LEFT for Lost Valley Ranch very early the morning after my birthday, so there was no time for my Nashville friends to celebrate with me. My girlfriends were super kind and reminded me as soon as I was home from the ranch that we would go to dinner. I have a few restaurants that I like to choose from when we're getting a real night together, and Virago is one of those.

Virago is a bougie sushi restaurant. Their amazing happy hour menu from 2012ish is gone, but my favorite things are still on the menu (or you can ask for them and they know): a crispy rice spicy tuna roll and a super sweet strawberry and champagne drink.

The girls and I piled into a booth, about eight of us total, and we all started talking too much and too fast and ordering rolls and drinks and edamame. As the meal came out in rounds, I asked them the same question Laura and I had been talking about. I asked if any of them had any hobbies.

In the group, we are mothers and wives and girlfriends and friends. We are employees and employers. We are homeowners and home renters. We are churchgoers and church skippers.

But that question silenced us.

No one had an answer.

No one had a hobby.

Some gals started stammering out some words, so I pulled out my phone and started taking notes. I was fascinated. The theme was the same around the table. It was like we all forgot hobbies were an option, but when we started to think back, yeah, we wanted one. Ashley wants to grow vegetables like she used to pick with her grandmother. She talked about the tomato sandwiches they would make. Someone else mentioned fishing, a thing none of us have ever discussed or considered as a social activity. But something happens when you start letting your brain's Rolodex pull up the things that remind you of Eden.

Cooking.

Gardening.

Singing.

Fishing.

Within minutes, the words died down again and it seemed like everyone went somewhere else in their mind. Back to Eden. Back to love. Back to when being an amateur was a simple celebration of life. And I think we all felt it. That maybe there are ways we could be stitching things back together.

There is this opportunity, especially for people of faith, to partner with the God we serve to make things better on Earth. John Mark Comer writes about it in *Garden City*, but many pastors and teachers also talk about it a lot. We were always meant to create. To create with God, to take the natural resources on our planet and in our hearts and put them together to make something that brings life and flourishing to ourselves and our neighbors. I don't know this for sure, but maybe that was easier when people lived more slowly and more intentionally and didn't have Instagram. Maybe the days on the porch with my grandmother, snapping the beans, were building something I couldn't see.

By definition, hobbies are activities "done regularly in one's leisure time for pleasure."[1] We could chop that up and deal with each word: regularly, leisure time, pleasure. But you see them too. You can think long and hard about those words that describe a hobby.

I wonder when we lost them. I wonder when we quit choosing them. I wonder when we quit doing things regularly, for pleasure, for fun, in our leisure time. And I wonder, as I think about my own life, where my leisure time has gone.

But I do know this. I want it back.

Because I want to make a list of the things I can do that bring me joy and bring God glory. Things that may also sew little corners of the world back together.

THE LIST LAURA was making while we sat at Neighbors isn't short. It's full of things she wants to make time for. Things she wants to fit into her schedule and her life. All things that pay nothing. In fact, they all cost something in time, and many cost something in money. But they all put the world back together in some way. Here are a few examples.

Take piano lessons
Learn to dance (take dance class)
Skydive
Scuba dive
Hang glide

Learn about wine and deep origins
Take a cooking class
Go to an improv night
Start a girl band
Join a book club

Now that last one is something I know about.

# Book Club

I'VE BEEN A READER my whole life and a fan of Oprah for almost as long. I remember when her television show was one not to be missed. It was on at my house every day at 4:00 p.m. EST. My babysitter would be watching when I got off the bus from school, and I would slide down on the couch with a snack in hand and watch with her. Then in 1996, Oprah made us all want to be in a book club.

I have been committed to two book clubs, and I loved them both. One in each city I've lived in. One in each decade of my grown life.

The one in my twenties began one fall when the leaves were changing and a group of my girlfriends went to a lake house in North Georgia for the weekend. As we all sat around on squishy couches with cups of coffee on Saturday morning, Nan casually began talking about the books she was reading and I was impressed. Classics. Modern popular novels. Fiction. Nonfiction. The books she listed ran the gamut of literature. When I asked how she picked them and why, she mentioned that she was reading them all for her book club.

I didn't know anyone in a book club (except Oprah). I peppered her with questions. When did they meet, how often, who picked the books, when did it start? And then I sheepishly asked if I could come sometime.

She said yes immediately and told me the book to grab for that month. I got it from my favorite local bookstore as soon as we got back to town and I started to read. I didn't want to mess this up. It felt like a big deal. I was in my midtwenties; Nan and her friends were in their midthirties. I felt very mature and grown up to be reading along with women who were most definitely adults.

The first meeting was a discussion about a nonfiction faith-based memoir. The second month, we read a novel.

Y'all would have laughed at me if you'd seen me during the second book club night. The gorgeous house we went to belonged to a family of five. Candles were lit throughout the home, coffee was brewing, and rosewater cookies (right out of our novel) were fresh out of the oven. Like, the host had actually found a recipe for the cookies in the book and made them AND I DID NOT KNOW THAT WAS EVEN AN OPTION.

I knew that very night these were the kind of women I wanted to be. Their houses were more grown up, with husbands and rugs and garage doors that opened automatically—all things I wanted. I was different from them, but somehow when we all read the same book, I was one of them.

As the youngest member, I sometimes chose to sit back and observe because I felt I had little good to offer the conversation. Now, as a woman in my thirties who spends a pretty significant amount of time with men and women in their twenties, my gracious, what I would say if I could go back and talk to that Annie in that book club. I'd tell her about her value to a room of women who miss the days when life was grown up but a little simpler. I would tell her that the mere fact that they invited her is enough for her to be confident there. (No one pity invites to a book club.) I would tell her that there is something so refreshing about filling a room with a variety of experiences and ages, and in a room full of late-thirties women, it can feel like we are all just tired, even if we read the whole book. But I couldn't have known all of that then, and it's better not to know maybe. These book club women had busy lives, inside their homes and out, but I admired how they would take time to sit together, with a mug of coffee or a glass of water, and discuss the intricacies of literature.

My twentysomething peers and I were meeting up too. But we were meeting at Starbucks on Saturday morning to read and share magazines and make a plan for Saturday night and discuss our Fridays. It was, um, different. Sometimes regrets were shared and sometimes we overslept and sometimes it just felt like a version of college without classes. These book club women didn't read the latest romance novel on the bestseller list or sit at Starbucks and try to write the ending to the romance novels we thought we were living. These grown-up women wanted to read the classics, the heart-wrenching nonfiction pieces, the fiction novels, and the historical works that I would never pick out for myself.

The women in my book club were so wise too. I was amazed at their knowledge, depth, and insight. They spoke eloquently, they thought deeply, and they related it all back to their love of God and love of family. And that would always do something to my insides.

So as much as I loved the book club itself, I think it was more about being in a room with these women once a month, talking about a book I loved reading, but mostly listening to the ladies who were smarter than me. They gave me that certain type of feeling. You know it too. You can feel it when you hear, read, or see something that so amazes you that your insides tighten up and you feel like you are breathing a new type of air.

I was in that book club for years, until I moved to Nashville. At the last meeting I attended, the women gifted me with books and hugs. It meant so much to me, even though I still knew I was different. I still knew I was young. I still knew I was the one leaving for another city, but they sent me off as one would send off a cousin to a different life. I had learned so much, read so much, and loved every month when I got just a little more grown up and a little more mature and a little more thirtysomething for the three hours we met. I left that last night hoping that someday, like my well-read friends, I'd be a smart book club member too.

I MOVED TO NASHVILLE and met Meg the first Sunday I was in town. She told me she was reading *Eat, Pray, Love* for a book club, and it almost brought tears to my eyes. The connection I had grown to love at the book club back home made me absolutely salivate at the idea of finding a book club so quickly in Nashville.

My original book club was full of women I had known up close and from a distance my whole life; this Nashville book club was absolutely swimming with strangers. I had never seen most of the faces before that first night in August when we sat outside on a porch and talked about a book I had devoured. (Everyone had.) I couldn't believe I was already in some sort of group. I had only lived in Nashville for a few weeks and here was a collection of women making space for me when they gathered around a story—again. Here was a group in which I wasn't sure I would fit, but they said I did, so I believed them—again.

We read different books from the first book club I was in. There were a few faith selections, but we leaned far more on modern fiction. One woman would pick the book for the next month and host. As that year carried on, the books we read were always choices I would have never found on my own. I loved most of the books. I read most of them all the way through, but I always showed up, even if I hadn't finished. (When you're new to town, you show up when invited if you want to make friends. Even if you haven't read the book.)

As the months and years passed, book club was a constant. I got to host a few times, and the first time I did, I dove back into the book club folder in my mind and knew I needed a recipe from the book. So I called our favorite local bakery and got a cake made, just like the one in the book. It had real flowers as decorations and everything. I wasn't the guest; I was the host. I wasn't the new girl; I was welcoming the new girl who had just moved to town. I wasn't the youngest in the room; I was the thirtysomething woman hosting in my home, candles lit and beautiful plates out on the table. The throw pillows on the couch were fluffed, and I wasn't rushed before the women all arrived. I had become the women I watched a decade before, in a different city and a different time.

I didn't know hobbies did that, but this one did. The longer I practiced this hobby, the more I saw myself becoming who I wanted to be. Not only were my hosting skills improving (which I totally think is a skill for men and women, not something just naturally born into all of us) but I was reading so much. I've always loved to read, but something is different when you aren't the only one deciding what book to pick up. I was being stretched and taught by the books and by the women who sat around the dining room table or on the living room couches and talked about what we read.

I was looking in the mirror at the woman I wanted to be a decade ago.

BUT LET ME also tell you the truth about our Nashville book club.

It died.

I don't know why. I don't even remember the last meeting or why we never scheduled another one. I just know that at some point in the last few years, we stopped meeting. Even though we had close to twenty women the month we read *The Help*, it's all gone now. And I miss it desperately.

I wish I could remember the last book we read or the reason we never met again. I see a few of the women very frequently; they are some of my best friends. At random moments we will say that we miss book club, but no one picks a book or sends an email. We just miss it. I wonder if it all stopped the same way every other hobby stops. The leisure time disappears or the things we do for pleasure get put on the back burner, then suddenly we blink and a highlight of our every month is out of our lives.

So weird.

For something we all loved, for something I had come to consider a tent peg in my Nashville life, for a night I always looked forward to and planned things around, it's weird to think it is just gone. But it is. And I'm not sure I could resurrect it. And I guess on the other hand, if I really wanted to, I would have. So I guess I need to look at that woman in the mirror too—the one who let book club die and isn't doing the work to bring it back.

IT'S BEEN YEARS since I've had a traditional book club in my life. But that's because I've started something new. It's very small and sweet, but I'm telling you, it's just like a book club. It's only three of us, it's over lunch, and it's every other month. The pressure is low and the commitment is even lower, but we really care. We are reading works that are hard to read: things about racial injustice and the mistreatment of our environment. We are reading books by authors who aren't the same race as we are or in the same phase of life. We are reading fiction and nonfiction, but we're reading with purpose.

And it's another level of interesting and intentional and fun. It's a different thing. I have long passed grown-up status, but I continue to refine and make it better. This book club doesn't show me grown-ups. It doesn't make me feel like a grown-up. It's proof that I am a grown-up and proof that I'm working to be better.

I hope this book club will last. I hope this one has some distance to it. But maybe one of the things I love about book club is it isn't forever. I never knew it wasn't, but now I do.

And when you learn that, you love it differently. So I'm loving this book club differently.

It's a hobby that is growing me and maybe, just maybe, reading books and talking about them will put the world back together in some little way. Or, at least, it will give me the words to try to teach myself how to do it.

Maybe hobbies are also moments along your path that tell you who you were and who you are and who you want to be. Maybe you're like me and they mark growth within yourself and your community and with God.

And I wonder if you're reading this book in a book club? I sure hope so.

# Tim's House

TIM SHAW is a very good friend of mine. A former NFL player, Tim was diagnosed with ALS a few years ago, and it has radically changed his life. This man who used to run around the football field now uses a wheelchair in public and has little use of his arms and legs. He used to chat up a storm and even do some freestyle rapping every now and again, but now he says only a few words and those are often slurred.

His main form of communication these days is an incredibly smart computer screen. He can look at the screen, and it will recognize where his eyes go on a visible keyboard and type out what Tim wants to say. He looks to the button that will make the computer speak, then whatever Tim's mind thought and his eyes typed is read in a robotic voice to all of us in the room.

A few weeks ago, when Tim, our friend Melinda, and I were hanging out in Tim's living room, we tried to come up with a name for his robot voice, but the system he uses comes with a few different voices and each is already connected to a name. Alfonzo, Karen, Thomas, etc. Tim has picked the most professional accent-neutral voice. His name is James, and he is definitely not the most entertaining of the options. It is significantly more hilarious when Tim uses Karen's high-pitched female voice or Thomas's very deep southern drawl. There are also other language options but the fear of changing it all to a language none of us knows and then not being able to change it back made the curiosity not worth it. But playing around with the different voices reading Tim's thoughts had us all dying laughing.

Because of ALS, everything in my current friendship with Tim is a bit slower than the rest of my life. When I ask him a question, I then sit in the chair across from him and wait as he looks from letter to letter, typing words into a sentence that will, in a few seconds, be read to me, hopefully by Karen or Thomas but most likely by boring robot James.

Tim and I used to meet for coffee to hang out, but when it became more difficult for him to drive himself around town, I started going over to his house instead. I don't remember how it started, but one day Tim decided that he would teach me how to play chess. It always felt like a game that was out of my reach mentally, but Tim promised he'd be able to teach me and that it would even be fun. It also gave us a thing, you know? A thing we did that was an easy connection point, something intentional that doesn't revolve around eating or drinking or doing anything active.

Like many of us, I'm fairly proficient at checkers, but chess is a totally foreign game to me. There are so many different pieces that move in different ways—it's confusing. But I really love the power and swag of the queen. There's so much strategy and so much to memorize. Because Tim's arms do not lift and his hands cannot grasp things anymore, it's on me to listen closely to him and move his piece as he instructs, and then for me to respond with my move. It usually isn't the computer telling me the moves to make for Tim; it's Tim himself. In a quiet room with no ambient noise, if Tim has the energy, he can speak and be pretty easy to understand. So as we started playing, Tim would teach me and instruct me, still always managing to beat me. (He has never once, not one time, taken it easy on me.)

CHESS IS VERY HARD TO PLAY. That's what I'd mostly like to say about that. Even in my smartest moments, I haven't played enough to be good. It takes a lot of time and practice and lots of sitting down at the board to get very good. And Tim is very, very good. The problem for me, and I think this highlights a bigger problem in my life in general, is that I'm mostly concerned about the next move, the one right in front of me, not the one three plays from now. Tim says you always have to be thinking three moves ahead in order to win. Well, gracious, my brain can't do that because I have to handle the one that is right in front of me first! I'm barely remembering which pieces go which way as it is—much less how to move those same pieces three moves from now.

But Tim always does. He always thinks that far ahead. And I can see it in his eyes as he looks down at the board for forty-five seconds, and I look at his face as his eyes get the tiniest little glimmer. One time in particular, after the glimmer showed up, he looked up at me and then started looking at his super smart computer screen. I figured he was typing a sentence to say to me. But suddenly, the speakers of the computer started playing "End of the Road" by Boyz II Men and Tim began to laugh. And then he told me the move he wanted me to make for him—the move that would absolutely be checkmate—and I was done for. He is ruthless and easily humored by his own jokes.

It's actually an excellent tool for teaching chess, to get to move the pieces for both sides of the game. For example, if Tim says "Rook to C4," I look down and as I move that piece, I'll say, "Wait, tell me why you're doing that." Sometimes he'll teach me but other times he'll just move his eyebrows up and down a few times and laugh. And then Boyz II Men gets cued up and I'm in big trouble.

LEARNING CHESS has been really good for me. Especially learning from Tim. I tend to run my life, and my fun, at an incredibly fast pace, which you may have guessed about me by now. Hurry to this, buzz through that, finish this thing so you can get to THAT. The slow pace of the game, the quiet of the room while one of us, or the other, thinks through the next move, has not only slowed me down but it has also slowly softened something in me. I come to rest while we play. I feel the muscles in my face and neck relax. I start to notice things around the room and outside I haven't seen before. As I'm sitting and waiting for Tim's move, studying the board, studying my friend, studying the breeze in the trees behind the pool, I'm learning to have fun slowly.

LAST CHRISTMAS we got my dad a really nice chess set. I don't know how in my forty years on the planet I had never heard (or listened to) this fact about my dad—he really loves to play chess. It was a hobby of his as a child and teenager. He used to read books about chess and play it often, but he hasn't made a habit of playing it in the last few decades of his life. (Probably because he was working full-time and had a wife and kids and, like many of us, gave up his childhood hobbies in exchange for an adult life.) So as I got into chess, and my mom reminded us that Dad really loves that game, all the kids in our family decided to get him a custom-made board and some nice weighted metal chess pieces. He was excited—we could tell as soon as he opened the gift—and it wasn't long before the pieces were set up.

I immediately offered for us to jump into a game. I figured it would be fun to use the skills I had gained from getting clobbered by Tim to play with my dad. I was surprisingly nervous because it felt like meeting a side of him I didn't already know.

Being a grown-up with parents can set up weird moments like this, where you realize for the first time that your parents, while raising you, were just normal adults (like you are now). I notice things about my life today and think back to when my parents were this age and I remember those years well. I just turned forty myself, and I clearly remember both my parents' fortieth birthday parties. (Life is weird, man.) I try to look back on those stories through the lens of knowing what it feels like to be that age adult. It's kind of trippy, honestly. And then moments like this chess game happen and not only do I feel like I have these glimpses of my dad as a fellow adult because I know some level of adulthood now but I also have moments where I feel like an adult seeing my dad as a child. Knowing what I know now, as an adult who relates to children, after learning about a part of my dad's childhood life, gives me a new view of him.

So as we sat across the chessboard from one another, setting up our pieces, I pictured his innocent and kind little mind learning a game that came naturally to him and his logical self as a child, and now playing it again. He told me, offhandedly, that he used to read books and magazines about how to play chess. And I thought of the 1960s kid-version of my dad reading those books. And I wished I could have known him. I think I would have liked being his friend.

The game started off simple enough, and it was slow and quiet, just like with Tim. I was hopeful for that, more than I think I knew to express. I wanted this to be slow. To be savored. To carry some of the peace that I find across the board from Tim as well. It was different not to be moving both sides of play. It actually made me pay closer attention and watch every move. Dad made a few early suggestions, reminding me of who goes first and correcting me on my very first move. I told him I did not want to cheat, but he strongly suggested that I rethink that first move and then explained that if we went forward as we were, he would have me beat in three moves.

That felt embarrassing, so I decided to cheat rather than be embarrassed. ☺ I backed my guy up and made a different move. So instead of my dad beating me in three moves, he beat me in six.

I was stunned at his brilliance. I have always found my dad to be extra smart, but this was next level. He checked into something when he sat down at the board that I did not know lived in him. He was always kind, never incredibly competitive, and he always quietly played his next move. Then he'd sit back in his chair, rest his forearms on his thighs, interlock his fingers, rub his thumbs together, and wait on me to move right into whatever trap he had laid. I yelled to the rest of our family, "Wait, did y'all see that?!? Dad just destroyed me!" I'm sure my eyes were as big as saucers. He kindly smiled and asked if I wanted to set up the board and go again. And of course I did, mainly because I just wanted to watch him do that again. And I wasn't done playing.

I knew the chances of ever beating him were slim, but I knew the chances of being with him were really high if I said yes again. And that's what I love about playing chess with Tim too. It is fun and all, but it mainly makes space for connection and time. Fun often breeds that. There's something specifically good and maybe holy about the slowness of this particular game and the way it stretches time.

Slow hobbies are good hobbies. In fact, the more I think, the more I cannot come up with a hobby that is rushed. Fishing is slow and requires patience until you get the fish on the hook. Crocheting a scarf cannot be rushed; it is done stitch by stitch. You cannot force a cake to be baked any quicker than the clock moves. Rock climbing requires slow and thoughtful decision making.

A theme I am feeling in my life, in my faith life, in my relationship life, and in my hobby life is that slow is better. Slow is good. For all the moments I want love at first sight, there is just something about the beauty of falling in love slowly and practicing hobbies slowly and living life slowly.

I've always found fun by going fast, but what if I've actually been missing the most fun because the rush mattered more to me? Tim is teaching me that in chess. But he's also teaching me that in life.

ON THE SATURDAY morning of the Walk for Life in Nashville, the rain made it impossible to hold the event outside. So the hundreds of people in attendance were corralled into the university arena instead of out on the football field and track. A lot of teams were there supporting different friends and family members who are affected by ALS. After the awards ceremony happened and all the announcements were finished, the walk started. Since we were in a basketball arena, we just lapped the concourse, passing the concession stands and bathrooms over and over. Ashley, Chris, and I were walking together, toward the end of the pack, and as the concourse curved left around the corner of the basketball court, there was Tim's wheelchair with his talking computer screen attached. But no Tim.

The pace slowed a bit as some sort of traffic jam was occurring. We all slowed to an almost stop. Through the crowd ahead, I could see Tim's mom and dad walking with their arms around each other's waists. And about four rows of people in front of them, I saw two of Tim's brothers with Tim in the middle. Being held up by his armpits, one brother on each side, Tim was sliding one foot and then the other. It had been months since I'd seen Tim walk, and here we were, all following his lead, his pace, his walking. It felt a little like Tim had handed ALS a checkmate right then and there, reminding the disease that it doesn't get to pick the pace or win every game.

# TPAC

I LOVE MUSIC. That won't surprise anyone who listens to the podcast or knows that I live in Nashville, aka Music City, USA. (And, FYI, if you're gonna call our town by a nickname, stick with Music City over NashVegas. NOBODY here likes NashVegas. I will put it in writing and speak for the millions of people who live here. We don't like it. Amen.)

I've been singing for as long as I can remember. I got a church hymnal in third grade and bought a tiny three-octave keyboard and a beginner's book for playing piano at Jennings, the local music store. I went to a public middle school where everyone who wants to be in the band or the orchestra gets a chance to do so. I remember struggling to decide between trying the French horn in the band or the cello in the orchestra. (Honestly, though, they both kind of play the same role in a performance or a piece of music.) In the end, I chose the French horn. More of my friends were in the band and being with them sounded fun to me, so French horn it was.

I dove all in—I'm sure that shocks you—and I loved it immediately. I practiced at home, which drove my family absolutely crazy. I took private lessons across town in a woman's tiny house sitting on a piano bench, always nervous because I had never practiced as much as she wanted me to. I worked incredibly hard to be the best player in my band class. I "challenged" the players who got ahead of me in seating. I spent three years of my life playing that instrument and absolutely loved it.

But I quit when I went from middle school to high school for what I now consider the world's dumbest reason: my friends said it wasn't cool. I remember where we were sitting when two girls told me I should pick another activity in high school because playing the French horn wouldn't be cool.

After all that practice, all that love, all those concerts and rehearsals and hours spent with that instrument, I never held one again. It still makes me sad. I made the wrong decision.

I'VE ALWAYS BEEN a fan of live theater. I grew up getting to see shows at the Fox Theatre in Atlanta. It is extraordinary. The inside looks like the most royal scenes from *Aladdin*— the ceiling reflects the Middle Eastern sky with sparkling stars across a stretch of navy blue, the carpet is beautifully bright red, and the room is full of gold. The stage is big and bright and bordered in gold as well. It's probably one of the most elegant rooms I've ever been in. Gold lanterns and gold tassels decorate the whole place from front to back. We went a few times as a field trip with my public school. We would see movies played on the big screen after singing along with the antique organ, and every now and then, I would get to see a musical with my family.

At the start of the intermission of every show we saw, I would ask my parents if I could walk down to the orchestra pit. They always said yes, and I would rush down there, lean over the edge, and scan the orchestra to find the French horn players. I would try to look at their sheets of music, see what type of mouthpiece they used, and watch them warm up or practice.

A FEW YEARS into my life in Nashville, I realized some of my friends were season ticket holders to our theater, Tennessee Performing Arts Center. I didn't even realize we had a theater, that we had Broadway shows come through town, or that we had a room that held the same shows that I could see at the Fox. I didn't have a full-time job for my first few years here, so things like being a season ticket holder at TPAC were way low on my list of financial priorities. But once things settled in my professional life, I jumped in.

My single season ticket is up in the balcony in the center of the second row. The couple of friends who have tickets the same night are down on the floor in the fancy seats, the kind of seats that include a pass to the fancy preshow party. But not me.

I prefer to sit in the balcony because I want to watch the orchestra. Specifically, I want to watch the French horn players. It brings something back for me to see the acting and singing on stage but also to look down and see the French hornists making magic and making music. It stirs two things in me at the same time, almost like oil and water. It stirs up joy and it also stirs up regret. If I would have stuck with it, would I be playing French horn professionally? I always wondered, back as a twelve-year-old, if I could do it as a job. So I watch the ones who didn't quit. I watch the ones who started playing one day when they were kids, just like me, and took private lessons, just like me, but kept playing because it's what they wanted. They didn't quit because some other middle schooler told them to.

WHATEVER YOU THINK is most fun, barring something illegal or enslaving or sinful, is the most fun for you and what you should put your time toward. You can like what you like. I wish someone would have said that to me in eighth grade. Maybe they did and I just didn't listen. But I think there was a deeper thing at play.

I cared most about being liked versus liking myself. I believed that if I did what everyone else wanted me to do, if I made choices that fell in line with what was believed to be cool, I would then feel like I was cool and therefore love being me. I had it absolutely all backward. I've learned that my favorite adults, my favorite kids, and my favorite friends are the ones who are so settled into who they are that they love what they love unashamedly. When you stop picking your hobbies or making decisions based on what others tell you is worth your time and effort, and you start listening to your own heart and your own wants, life gets so much richer.

I'm known for loving a few things in particular. Soccer. Glitter. Dolly Parton. Reba McEntire. Boiled peanuts. Nashville. *Wicked*. Kids. The French horn, obviously. And fun. I'm known for loving fun. Yet there was a time that isn't so far back in my history when I wasn't very public about what I loved. I've loved Dolly Parton and Reba McEntire since I was a child, but there was totally a time where I wouldn't have talked about that love as publicly as I do now, because I would worry about what you, whoever the "you" is, would think. Because how I felt about me was determined by how you felt about me.

I thought this was mostly a female problem until some of my close male friends started saying similar things. Body and self-hate issues and questions about what others think of them. They experience the same insecurities I feel on a daily basis, but theirs are wrapped up with some masculinity questions that I am not asking in my life. These things are a problem for all of us. We all question if we are enough, or if we are too much, or if what we have to offer the world is what the world really wants.

I REALLY LOVE nineties country. I've loved country music my whole life. My parents often tell a story of tiny Annie, small enough to still be in a car seat, with my headphones on and Dolly Parton music in my ears, singing "Workin' 9 to 5" at the top of my lungs. My teenage years were spent at the family lake house, laying out on the dock, with country music playing from 101.5 FM on our radio. I've been a country music fan as long as I've been an Annie. My parents raised me right.

And I've often said that if I could pick any time to be an adult in Nashville, I would have picked the late nineties. Having peak songs from Alan Jackson and The Chicks (formerly known as the Dixie Chicks) and Shania Twain and Garth Brooks and Clay Walker and bootcut jeans and barely any internet feels like a dream.

So when my friend Annie Parsons sent a text to our crew of girlfriends, Jennifer and Kelley and me, inviting us to a nineties country concert with a bunch of our favorite artists? WHAT AN EASY YES.

When the night of the show arrived, a Monday night in the fall, it had been a long few days. The week before had been full of stress and loss. It was one of those weeks that felt LONG. And like when I saw the Downton Abbey movie in the middle of the day with Heather, I needed to escape again. I wanted to fall back into something fun that I knew and something that reminded me of back then and back there. I wanted a glimpse of Eden.

So when Dave Barnes and his friends decided to do an entire show of nineties country, it felt like it could be that again—a return to something I missed about my childhood, songs that raised me and taught me and of which I knew every word.

Other Annie, who had bought the tickets and reserved a table, had gotten us the VERY FRONT and CENTER table below the stage at one of our favorite venues: 3rd & Lindsley. This was hilarious to me because it meant Dave could literally look down from stage and I was right there. So many of the musicians performing that night were our friends, and to see us right there, front and center, made everyone laugh. But the funny thing is the whole room was full of our friends because every single person in our friend group had been looking forward to this night.

We sang a million favorites—"Goodbye Earl," "Neon Moon," "How Do I Live without You," "Just to See You Smile." The list went on and on for a couple of hours. And the whole crowd, your Annie included, sang along at the top of our lungs.

I didn't even consider what other people were thinking about my singing or my tearing up or my huge every-tooth-visible smile. And when all the artists came out at the end, Claire Dunn leading the way, to sing "Strawberry Wine," it was like we were transported somewhere else—exactly where we wanted to be. And for just a couple of minutes, we got to rest there, laugh there, and sing at the top of our lungs. I had the best time.

I got what I went there for because I allowed myself to be myself: fully me, sing-along me. It's taken me almost four decades, but hopefully that leaves five more decades at the minimum for me to love what I love, sing along to the songs that remind me of a simpler time, and like the lyrics from Rascal Flatts's song "Mayberry." I hope it also gives me plenty of time to get good at playing the French horn again. Because, you know what? That sounds fun.

# Alliance Soccer Complex

I'VE HEARD ABOUT something called a runner's high. I've heard how it matters for a woman's body that has been diagnosed with PCOS to move and sweat. But exercise has never been fun for me in a way that sticks. I hike fairly often at Radnor Lake and I go to a workout class called b.fab.fitness, but it's never a long-term love.

Because of PCOS, which again stands for polycystic ovary syndrome, my body doesn't change much when I exercise. That can be frustrating because of a lot of weird baggage I have about the purpose of exercise and the size a body should be and how one begets the other. We are in a beautiful time in culture where body differences for women are more understood and accepted. Diet culture is losing some grip on the minds of people, but that doesn't totally undo all the things I learned and thought and heard as my body was maturing. So, sadly, some of that baggage exists and it doesn't make exercise all that fun for me.

When we recorded an episode of our *EnneaSummer* series, Enneagram coach and expert Seth Abram mentioned how each Enneagram number has a different type of exercise and way of eating that works best for it. I had never thought about that, but I googled it as soon as our conversation was finished.

Enneagram Sevens need to play, it told me. The idea clicked immediately. My mind jumped back to a younger time in my life, a time when a soccer ball was never far from my feet, when rolling around on grass and slide tackling and chasing other players and the ball was the most fun I could have.

At the time we were recording that episode, I hadn't played in a game since high school. Two full decades. But suddenly I knew what was missing from my exercise life— fun from sports. I wasn't having the kind of fun that felt connected down to my bones and down through my history. And I hadn't had that level of fun in exercise since the end of my senior year of high school.

There are challenges to being a grown-up, and part of those challenges is that adding responsibilities often costs fun or costs hobbies (like my dad with chess, though clearly he's still got it). We only have so many hours in a day and so much to get taken care of and often fun feels like this luxury and bonus that's not worth making time for or carving out a way to keep in our schedules. Exercise had become a chore in my life. It was always an exchange, never a gift.

But soccer had always been a gift to me. It was hard, I wasn't THE VERY BEST at it when I was a teenager, and there were times I quit when I should have persevered. But I loved it. I loved the team aspect, I loved the beauty of the game, and I loved watching the ball in motion.

But what does that mean for me today?

THROUGH TIM, I met Stacey. Stacey and Tim met when Tim was playing football, and now Stacey was the trainer for the Nashville Soccer Club, Nashville's professional soccer team. I had been to parties and meals and church with Stacey before, but I had also watched him on the sidelines of soccer matches. So I shot him a little text on a Wednesday, and we met up for coffee on Friday.

I teared up just as we sat down. I explained to Stacey how much I missed soccer. I told him how exercise was never a great thing for me but sports always were and are. I told him how I needed fun and how soccer was always fun, and then I asked him to make me a soccer player again.

He smiled because he's very kind, and he said he could do that.


I WAS TEN MINUTES late for my first session. I ran into the bathroom of the massive gym and changed and jumped out and found Stacey. The gym is split into three sections: volleyball, basketball, and soccer. The soccer area is covered in turf and Stacey had laid out little cones on the ground with a soccer ball in the center. I took a deep breath and stepped forward.

An hour later, covered in sweat and red-faced, tears dripped from my eyes. I cried because that hour was SO FUN. I cried because my foot connecting with a soccer ball is also my guts connecting with something more—with middle school Annie and with those outside games and the smell of the grass and the sound of a shoe sending a ball downfield. I was back there and I was happy.

It's all about connection anyways, isn't it? With God, with others, with ourselves—yesterday and today.

My first day of soccer wasn't easy. In fact, I felt a little bit like a fish out of water in some ways. It had been so long since I kicked a ball, besides playing in the backyard with the Barnes kids. I've watched hours of soccer on television or from a seat in a stadium, but the footwork is very different when it's your own two feet and they are the feet of an amateur.

HOBBIES AREN'T ALWAYS going to be easy. Fun isn't always easy. But those words, *fun* and *easy*, aren't synonymous.

Pretty regularly at soccer practice (that's what I call it), Stacey makes me do this very intricate footwork pattern that is really hard for me. I do not, for the life of me, understand why my brain cannot get around taking the ball from my right foot and pulling back and sending it, like an L, behind my left leg, and then using my left foot to grab it and pull it back to the center. I'm usually not in a great mood about it. We've practiced this same move for weeks and I still can't get it and he keeps making me do it even though I STILL CANNOT GET IT. I don't want to get mad at Stacey, but I don't know where to channel my frustration.

I haven't quit, and I don't want to. When Stacey and I were chatting at the start of yesterday's practice, before I was too exhausted to talk, we realized we are the exact same age (though I'm TECHNICALLY nineteen days older than him). After we came to that realization, he asked me an interesting question. "If you could go back and be any age, what would you pick?" I think he said it would only be for a month. I asked him if I got to take my current knowledge with me and he said yes. Then I knew right away. I would go back to being fourteen in a heartbeat. I would go back to my freshman year of high school.

Maybe it was partly due to my proximity to a soccer ball and the connection it makes me feel, but I wanted a shot at that first year of high school again, especially with what I know now about my spiritual future, my body's future, and my heart's future. I would go right back there and hope it was during soccer season.

I don't believe in regrets, really. I think there is something to be learned from everything we experience, but I can trace back to a couple of defining moments that absolutely shaped the rest of my life—in both positive and negative ways. One that happened my freshman year was a moment where I quit on a soccer drill when I could have, and should have, kept going. And I know that shaped my sporting future, but it also shaped my life and made quitting an option that I never really wanted to have. I've learned to persevere (you can read about that in *Looking For Lovely*), but it is a journey I could have done differently if I wouldn't have quit that day as a freshman.

If I could go back, I would tell myself about the fun that comes from being strong in your body and in your mind. I would run as fast as I could. I would play every minute of every game that was scheduled that month and I would smile from start to finish. I would hug some of my high school friends whom I know, twenty years later, aren't even a part of my life. I would pay more attention in history class and I would read every book assigned. And I would hurry down to that band director's room and I would ask for a tryout, just to see if he had space for me in the French horn section.

I would make decisions about hobbies that would stick for the rest of my life.

IT'S BEEN A FEW MONTHS since I started playing soccer again, and I can tell that my skill level is returning and is maybe more precise than even when I played in high school. I haven't been late again like I was that first day because my schedule shifted when soccer came back into my life. Everything was moving so fast that I would buzz into every meeting, skip out on exercise because I "didn't have time," and set alarms at meals with friends so we knew when I had to leave. But then I decided that soccer needed to win because everything needed to slow down.

I sat with a friend a few days ago and she said, "You show what matters most by what you say yes and no to, by who gets your time and your money." It really made me think—about hobbies, about friendship, and about the speed at which I'm living my life.

WHEN CHEF MELISSA D'ARABIAN came on the podcast (episode 167), I was a little starstruck. I've been a fan of her cooking on Food Network for years and then there she was, sitting across the desk from me. Once the conversation got going, my pulse slowed down and my mind slowed down and we just got to know each other.

That's the whole trick of my podcast. That's the secret sauce. I try to forget there is a microphone and just pretend we are two people sitting at coffee trying to get to know each other or, if we are already friends, just having a convo to catch up.

So in the process of getting to know Melissa, I listened as she talked about beef stew. Her mother-in-law taught her an intricate and time-consuming recipe for the most delicious beef stew she had ever eaten, but it wasn't fast. Each ingredient had to be handled separately and purposefully. It is one of those recipes that could take most of your day, but the payoff is an insanely delicious and layered experience.

I'm a person who wants to enjoy the experience of eating as much as I enjoy the food. I like fancy restaurants not because I am bougie (okay, not ONLY because I'm bougie) but because of how they've thought through the entire experience the guest is going to have. But the experience of cooking a meal is often more enjoyable than the eating of it. Cooking is medicine, right?

That's how hobbies work. The making of the thing is just as rewarding, if not more so, than the actual product. I think back to times when women held quilting bees. They would sit around working on a quilt, talking, laughing, and sewing. The finished quilts were necessary and important for whoever received them, but the real good stuff was what happened around that circle. It's true in book club too. I don't necessarily want the book to end or the book club meeting to end, I just want to be in the middle of both. I don't need to play in a soccer league or be recruited by the US Women's National Team (but y'all know how to find me if you're looking for a defender), I just love practicing.

Remember, a *hobby* is defined as an activity "done regularly in one's leisure time for pleasure." And I don't know that I actually have one anymore.

But I need one. I really need a hobby.

I need a hobby so that I don't treat social media like a hobby. Scrolling is not a hobby.

I need a hobby so there is space in my day, or my week, to cultivate leisure time and use it wisely.

I need a hobby because hobbies connect people and I want to feel that connection.

I need a hobby because I miss Eden and there just seems to be something about the power of making a thing, creating a thing, putting time into an activity, that may remind me and give me a taste of what I long for.

So that's why I went back to soccer—because it feels like Eden and it seems that I can almost find my way back with the ball at my feet.

And you need a hobby too.

You need a hobby because you need space.

You need space in your life because you need connection.

Scuba diving with my people STEPHANIE | Walks with husband, son & with family EMILEE | Outdoor adventuring with friends DANIELLE | CHRISTINE | Coffee with friends JESSICA | Being with my kids | Crafting with my friends SARAH | Morning with Aaron & Gigi RACHEL | Lake days behind a boat | Moon River Music Festival with my friends trip HANNAH | A living room dance party MIRANDA | Girls' trip with sister, Brianne charades BECCA | Tubing at the lake CARRIE | Dancing to yummy food MEGAN | Yarning with coffee and Netflix SAM | band concerts at Disney World RACHEL | Mountain hikes NIKKI | Swing dancing at Lake Robbins MELANIE | A day at the porch sunset TAMMY | Anywhere with my three boys STACY | Windows down. Music up. BRITTA | Baking cookies with my Traveling Europe with my wife THOMAS | Flying to New Zealand BREANNA | Chips & salsa & sunshine EMILY | Cozy coffee conversations with friends ADDY | to face. KATIE | Italy in summer with hubby DACY | Eat donuts on the beach AMY | Sipping Christmas chai White Russians RACHEL | Tiny house vacation in Alaska JEANETTE | Park day with my boys ADEENA | Hiking somewhere beautiful and new MICHELLE | to vinyl and napping MICHELLE | Eating tacos in Nashville MICHELENE | KATY | Going to concerts with friends HALEY | Coffee and Christy Miller audiobooks RACHEL | OLIVIA | Going to Disney World JESSI | Seven Tiny Oranges Reunion Tour CELIA | book, chocolate ASHLEIGH | Dance party with my kids JILL | Making bread, knitting, quilting VIRGINIA | MEGAN | Jeepy adventures with my people AVA | Cheering on the Dawgs GRACE | STEPHANIE | Finding my purpose GABRIELLA | Baking a fancy dessert TARA | ocean in Maine CORA | Being with my little family KAYCE | Chris, Lily, Ivy & Rosie WENDY | Fun times with big adventures EMILY | Taking a trip to Hawaii JANA | with my people DIANNA | Playing Skee-Ball down the shore EMILY | A really good book ABBY | Traveling Europe with daughter Ava TAMMY | Taking my son to Disneyland ALLISON | my kids thrive ANGELYN | Cake with lots of icing CASSANDRA | Dancing in Christmas masquerade ball ANNA ANGELA | husband CHERYL | Camper van and go SUSAN | Swimming in cavatappi noodles SARAH | college & getting a job ASHLEY | Opening a boutique for foster children ANGELA | birthday=Thanksliving ANDREA | A vacation somewhere beautiful MELISSA |

dog ASHLEY | Good coffee with good friends CAROLINA | Traveling the world Hammocking & reading with friends KRISTEN | Throwing pottery in my studio anywhere PAUL | Sparking joy for total strangers PAM | Libraries and spiral staircases HOLLY | beach walks with friends DIANNE | Scuba diving with family AMBER | Snuggling LAYNE | Making brown butter chocolate-chip cookies JESS | Disney World family/ people ALANA | Girlfriend getaway with yoga everyday BECCA | A living room LORYE | Quality time with quality people BRITTANY | Huge dinner parties with loud music KEARA | Time with my beagle, Lucy LAUREN | Games, friends, and Running an international marathon APRIL | Being at the beach CAYLA | Boy with my loves JENNY | Sitting on a beach reading BROOKE | Shopping with my sisters beach KRISTEN | Playing with my doggies CALLIE | Hanging out with family DONNA | Back Cooking for those I love JONATHAN | Snuggling with Tucker the dog BECKY | Driving. nephews SARAH | Car karaoke with friends RACHEL | Segway tour of new city LACEY | HILARY | Drinking tea with close friends KAITLIN | Crocheting, baking, and napping ADDY | Girls' trip to the beach KRISTEN | A vacation by a lake PAIGE | Seeing Jesus face to face. KATIE | Disney World with my family EMILY | Spontaneous living room dance parties HANNAHLEE | Sipping Christmas chai White Russians RACHEL | Campfire with s'mores and friends ABBY | Hiking in our national parks D'NITA | Park day with my boys ADEENA | Hiking somewhere beautiful and new HANNAH N. | Board games with my family SHARLA | Dance floor with live band KAYLA | Listening to vinyl and napping MICHELLE | Italy with all my people CARRIE | Beach vacation with my family MELISA | A Baylor football game KATY | Eating tacos in Nashville MICHELENE | Going to concerts with friends HALEY | Coffee and Christy Miller audiobooks RACHEL | Serving underprivileged kids in Belize TIFFANY | Sunshine and Disneyland OLIVIA | Going to Disney World JESSI | Seven Tiny Oranges Reunion Tour CELIA | Road tripping around Iceland JESSI | Being with my sisters KATIE | Bath, cabin, snuggles, MEGAN | Dance party with my kids JILL | Game night with my family DELANEY | Being a Young Life leader Jeepy adventures with my people AVA | Cheering on the Dawgs GRACE | Honey lattes with friends ANNA | Laughing until I cry DANIELLE | Thanksgiving-night movies Finding my purpose GABRIELLA | My friends all together, laughing BRIANNA | Back dive into the pool SUSAN | Walking along the Being with my little family KAYCE | Reading fireside, tea in hand SARAH | Crafting while listening to podcasts SARAH | Taking a trip to Hawaii JANA | Deep conversation with my people JORDAN | Acoustic JOHNNYSWIM at the Ryman STEPHANIE | Beach Hiking the beautiful Pacific Northwest MELANIE | Moving to a new state JEN | Hanging with friends MEGAN | Country drives with my husband CAITLIN | Watching my son to Disneyland ALLISON | Sun, sand, toes in water JILLIAN | Traveling with my Couch time with my boys CALI | Being able to cross-stitch CINDY | Graduating Podcasts and jigsaw puzzles TRISHA | Having a Mom Prom KATIE | Thanksgiving Playing and being Aunt Shannie SHANNON | Quiet mornings, books, cats, coffee MADELINE |

Biking. Hiking. Snowshoeing. Sewing. Singing. CAROLINE | Beach at sunset MELANIE | Game night with friends. Yay! ANNIKA | Snuggling with my son, Charlie JENN | Loch Lomond and Scottish Highlands ALEXANDRA | Buying a one-way ticket DIANA | Fresh coffee, front porch MEGAN | Coffee. Friends. Twinkling lights. Laughter. SHAUNA | Slow mornings & good books HANNAH | Disney World fireworks with family MIKA | Family, friends, serving God, Disney ASHLEY JEAN | Getting coffee with a friend NIKKI | Hiking with friends KATIE | Traveling with my husband, Cody KATHRYN | Traveling anywhere with my husband STEPHANIE | Date night with my husband AMIE | Spending life with Adam ELIZABETH | Going out for live music CHLOE | Running in the sunshine CHELSEA | Quiet time, podcasts, and coffee AVRIL | Decorating cookies with Jennifer Garner RACHEL | Lying under the stars NATALIE | Traveling with my fiancé CHLOE | Running in national parks CALLIE | Drinking coffee in the mountains AUDREY | Living overseas SHANNON | Being with my daughters and husband MELENE | Making hot chocolate bombs BETHANY | Sitting in rain with coffee JOCELYN | Hammock reading a good book GENEVIEVE | Books, books, books, and Kelly SHANNON | Books, books, books, and Shannon KELLY | Playing football, but just catch ANNIE | Driving the coast of Maine KAMALA | Running a marathon with friends CARROLL | Traveling the world by motorcycle BRITTANY | Visiting NYC at Christmastime LORI | Going for a hike KRISTEN | Seeing Wicked on Broadway LEXIE | Sun, beach, float, no plans JORDYN | Life together over ice cream ROBYN | Loving my best life MADISON | Taking a trip with family SUSAN | Sunny-day hiking with friends JULIA | CJ & Lily holding our miracle baby BETSY | Reading outside while son plays JOANNA | Hiking with my camera ROBIN | Partying like a hobbit ASHLEY | Playing with my friend's kids MARIAH | Brunch w/ friends and LEGOs w/ Ian SARABETH | Lightsaber battles with my son AIMEE | Family, Enneagram, food, books, relaxation JAYMEE | Puppy cuddles and afternoon naps BILLIE | Coffee with all my friends SAMANTHA | Blanket, book, tea, rainstorm KRISTIN | Travel and adventures for days KRISTEN | Entertaining around our kitchen island KAREN | Adventuring with my husband LAURA | Being in a Hallmark movie TAM | Traveling the world BECCA | Becoming a published author LATRICE | Mountains with my family DAWN | Picking blueberries EMILY | Board games and outdoor activities AMBER | Husband + pizza on the beach LYDIA | Song stories with Jon Foreman KATIE | Friends, family, games, food, tea BECKY | Drinking coffee with my sister MORGAN | Coffee on a cool morning KELLEY | European vacation with friends & family ERIN | Seeing what God is doing ANG! | Performing in musical theater LILLIAN | Day trips with my husband KATHERINE | LEGOs, dogs, traveling, tasty recipes JON(ATHAN) | Cooking by myself for people CLARA | Have a spa day HEATHER | Reading on the beach MELISSA | Rom-com movie marathon KIRBIE | Traveling/camping with my family KIM | Snuggling my granddaughters, Sonora & Mila JANA | Playing hooky with my daughter AMANDA | Outdoor fire with friends EMILY | Painting with Maggie and Molly KELLY | Creating healing art in community CANDIS | Exploring Ireland with coffee in hand ALLISON | Taking a week off to relax RONEL | Rock climbing with Annie F. Downs JESSICA | Snowshoeing in the Rocky Mountains SARA | Seeing a Broadway musical ABBY | Summertime stargazing, camping, paddleboarding RACHELLE | Independent mom-boss hustle time SAVANNAH | Disneyland with my people MEGAN | Learning new embroidery techniques JACQUI | Disney cruise with my family GABRIELLE | Meeting someone from every country SUMMER | Singing loudly in the car KAITLIN | Massage on Hawaiian beach CHERIE | Driving through mountains, autumn leaves JULIE | Skiing at Winter Park NICOLE | Playing games with friends DARCIE | Vacation away from cell coverage BECKY | Science-fiction TV and blankets MICHAL | Marrying my best friend ERICA | Hearing stories from grandparents EMMA | Traveling the world KRISTEN | A tea party with friends CASSANDRA | Snuggled up with Hallmark channel AMBER | Onstage singing KATHY | Hot tubs and comfort food MORGAN | Sleep. Coffee. Books. Friends. ADRIENNE | Walks around UGA's campus DANIELLE | Reading a brand-new book REBECCA | Finding community in my new city MINDY | Dancing until my feet hurt VICTORIA | New solo travel adventures AMANDA | Taco Party with my friends ALEX | Reading books & drinking tea JESSIE | Being with Taylor and Deidre ASTRI | Swimming and traveling in summer DEIDRE | Going on a long run LAUREN | Beach walks with the fam EMILY | Soccer on a Sunday night KATHLEEN | Know Christ; make Him known KATIE | Sabbathing in Maine with friends KATE | A train ride with girlfriends CYNDI | Reading in a hammock SHELBY | Cruise vacation with best friends MICHELLE | Dance party with my puppy CARRIE | Reading, lounging on the beach KATE | Mountain cabin, family, and coffee HANNAH | Hiking the Blue Ridge Mountains KAYLA | My house full of people KIM |

# Chase
*the* **Fun**

# Harvest House Porch

On a Tuesday in March, I watched the season finale of *The Bachelor* with a group of friends. We spread out on couches and sat on the floor and shared piles of french fries from Burger Up.

The next morning, one of those friends tested positive for COVID-19.

And before the week was over, I got a call from the health department and was told I had to quarantine in my house for ten days. This was at the very beginning of the United States' experience with the global pandemic that would shape our lives and our world for much of the year. But at the time, my friend was one of the first in our county to test positive, and therefore the health department was doing all they could to control the outbreak.

The phone call from the health department employee came on a Friday afternoon. "Are you home?" she asked once the hellos and nice to meet yous were out of the way. I told her I was not. She said, "Okay, well I need you to head home and plan to stay there for the next ten days. You cannot leave your house once you get there, but you are allowed to go outside and walk around the property of your home a couple times a day. I will be calling you each day to check in with you, ask you if you are having any symptoms, and have you take your temperature for me."

I was like a deer in headlights. Stay in my house? Alone? For ten days? No one coming in, no one (me) leaving. I couldn't imagine it.

I went home that night and ordered groceries. I called my parents and cried. Ten whole days. To some, that might feel like a gift of rest or an excuse to miss events you didn't want to attend in the first place. But for me? I didn't know how to do this.

I couldn't believe I had just spent the entire fall off the road, learning to find fun in my day-to-day life of not traveling for work but always being allowed to move around my life and my city. The new year had started off back to normal professionally. In fact, I had just finished two weeks on a tour bus traveling around and speaking. And then there I was, grounded again. Off the road again. Events canceled again. Back home again. But this time, not just home in Nashville. Home in Harvest House.

I was sad and afraid that first night. On top of the isolation, there was so much fear of the unknown with the disease. And I would be facing every hour alone. So I laid on the couch, sent a few texts canceling my weekend plans, and turned on the television. I let myself just melt into the couch and melt into whatever was on the screen. I don't remember falling asleep, but I woke up there the next morning.

And that day, once I had read my Bible and drank a strong cup of tea, I made a few decisions. I made a list of ways I could count down these ten days quarantined in my house.

I decided to wear a different color lipstick every day. I decided to count how many days I wore "real pants" (clothes I could wear to work) and "not real pants" (yoga pants, leggings, pajamas, etc.). I counted how many days I put on my glitter slippers.

And I made a bucket list. A quarantine bucket list. It included shows I wanted to watch and chores I had been putting off and books I needed to finish and new skills I wanted to learn (like juggling!).

In your knowledge of me and fun and the search for something that still feels like Eden, I'm sure you saw this coming, but I didn't feel like doing ANY of that. I didn't want to make fun out of this situation. I wanted to lay around and watch shows on television and just slog my way to day ten when I could go back out into the world. But I know myself. My friend Phil talks about knowing where the track is going before you get on a train, and I know how unhealthy I can get, in body and in mind, if the track laid down is a track of doing nothing. Wallowing in my isolation leads nowhere good—I don't like where that train goes.

So before I felt like having fun, I make a list of fun activities. Before I actually did one thing, I made a list of the things. And then I started checking them off. Work was based at home—I turned my guest bedroom into a podcast recording studio and my dining room table became my desk and video chat home base. I cooked every meal, never got behind on laundry, took my temperature a lot, and cried often because it still felt very lonely.

The ten days went by slowly, but they went by. But those ten days, as you well know, became months. Of course, the rules changed in my favor. Once the ten days were complete, I was allowed to go to the grocery store and a few other places, but I didn't go back to work for a while, restaurants didn't open, there were no sporting events to cheer at or concerts to attend. I was home far more than I ever imagined I would be. I think we all were.

During my quarantine, I found myself out on the Harvest House Porch a lot. Remember when I said I missed those evenings with the beans on the porch? Now a version of that, with many more worries and way less beans to snap, was right in front of me again.

Harvest House Porch is a small rectangle of cement just outside my living room. The furniture includes an L-shaped brown couch with white cushions, though they have faded to khaki as I never covered them and they've been exposed to the elements. I decorated the railing with multicolored Christmas lights and did not take them down after the New Year. But I was so glad for my holiday forgetfulness. I plugged those lights in every day of the quarantine, just for fun, because I was trapped, and it made me feel like it was a choice—that I was choosing to be in this beautiful place. I had meetings on the porch. I had meals on the porch. I sat on the front edge of my porch while friends drove by and waved or stopped and had a quick conversation.

For the first time since I bought this house, cleaning the porch became a part of my weekly rhythm. Between watching church and making lunch, I would dust off the table (springtime pollen is a real thing), rearrange the cushions, fold the blanket, and sweep the floor. And in the afternoons I would open the French doors, put an album on my record player, light a few candles, and sit outside and read. The Harvest House Porch became a place for rest, for work, for escape.

I WENT BACK to Lost Valley Ranch a few months into the pandemic, and some friends and I sat around a fire pit and talked about the quarantine and the stay-at-home orders that we had all experienced. My friend Jennie, a wife and mother of four, sat directly across from me. Flexing her arm muscles in the bonfire light, she said, "I bought a full set of weights, in case we end up spending more time in our homes. That's what I wished I had last time."

Our conversation started a round of questions in my mind.

What happens if THAT happens again? What if we need to be in our homes for an extended amount of time? What if all the traditional methods of finding fun—from hanging with friends to going to shows to eating at our favorite restaurants—continue to be out of reach and we have to make our own fun again?

How do we live an expansive life when the outside world might be limited?

The answers were all over Instagram and other social media platforms—families coming up with tons of activities in their homes, groups of friends setting up happy hours over video chat, puzzles being done in every home, videos galore of choreographed dances, kitchens being used more than ever before. At the same time, we all heard stories, or personally know someone who lost their battle with depression or anxiety. Many of us, myself included, struggled with our mental health, our emotional health, and even our spiritual health. Not gathering for church really took a toll on me, even though my church's online experience was amazing each week.

If I knew our world was changing and being home would continue to be a major part of my life, what would I do now to plan for fun, for joy, for an expansive life in a small (but special) condo in the middle of Nashville?

I called my friend Matthew who is a local contractor. He painted the walls and redid the floor of the Harvest House before I moved in. I asked him if he could come over to look through a home project I'd like to see completed. It was time to renovate the Harvest House Porch.

The side of the porch I share with my neighbors needed to be a full wall, not just a fabric partition. I wanted it a bit more closed off so that calls and conversations could be private. I wanted an outdoor television, just a small cheap one, so I could watch early morning soccer while drinking my tea. I wanted twinkly lights and better flooring and I wanted my furniture to be a bit more protected from pollen.

I received a full refund for a canceled trip that was planned during the pandemic, so I was able to put that money toward this renovation. I didn't even know the porch mattered that much to me until it was a lifeline. Until it was the most Eden-like place in my life.

As THE CONSTRUCTION on the porch began, I washed the cushion covers to make them white again. I took down the Christmas lights that had been up for seven months to make way for new twinkly lights. Matthew and I laid down new flooring and rearranged the furniture and hung some plants and suddenly, there was peace out on Harvest House Porch in ways I hadn't known. It's perfect now. No matter what culture or sickness or weather dictates next, I'm on the right path. I've created a porch that is a haven for me. It's a hub for lots of fun. And it reminds me of a porch I knew thirty years ago, the one where we snapped green beans, the one where there were no worries. I'm ready for all of that—beans and no worries—on this new porch too.

# Goodbye

IT MATTERS TO ME that you know I see you right here, all the way at the end of this book. You've done the work to read all the pages, hear all the stories, think through what fun might really look like in your life and how it could, maybe, connect you more closely to a God who really loves you.

Things don't always end the way you think they are going to. Relationships, books, football games, job opportunities, days at Dollywood. But the end doesn't get us to Eden anyway, does it? What makes life fun isn't the getting to where we are going; fun is in the going together. The rainbow, not the pot of gold. The soccer practice, not the end of the game.

Fun is right where you are. It is yours for the taking. Connection with God and connection with people, reminders of the best parts of your past and the dreams of your future, peace in the midst of a spinning storm and rest in the middle of a busy week.

So chase the fun, friend. Go after it. Find what sounds fun to you, and you will find what you are really looking for.

Maybe you will find it in the places where you are an amateur (aren't you glad to be an amateur!); maybe you will find it in love (I hope you are in love!); or maybe you'll find it in that hobby you just found or returned to.

And as I always say at the end of every episode, I think that's it for me today, friends.

If you need anything else from me, I'm embarrassingly easy to find.

Go out and do something that sounds fun to you, and I will do the same.

And we'll see you back here next time.

All my love.

# The Sounds
# of *That Sounds Fun*

As with every book I write, I tend to have music in the background at all times. As you listen to the *That Sounds Fun* podcast, you get to hear lots of musicians interviewed, and a few songs played as our background music every year. (We switch songs and artists about once a season, so approximately four times a year.) This book-writing process has been a little different, but there are still some artists/soundtracks/albums that have been very instrumental (LOL. SEE WHAT I DID THERE?) in helping me write this book and find this book and shape this book.

In no particular order, thanks to these artists. Y'all make sure to check out their music.

- Hozier
- *Poldark* soundtrack
- Jon McLaughlin, particularly his *Mood* albums

- Sleeping At Last, particularly his album *Atlas: Space* (*Deluxe*)
- Dolly Parton
- Dave Barnes, particularly his album *Carry On, San Vicente*
- Will Reagan
- *Hamilton* soundtrack (no one is surprised)

# Thank You

I WONDER HOW MANY of you started here, reading this section first. I always do. I like to know who and what gave energy and hope and relationship to an author in the middle of an incredibly challenging journey from start to finish of a book project. My list is always long. I am so very aware of how I am unable to do any good thing in my life without incredible people around me.

Downs Books Inc., *That Sounds Fun* podcast, and That Sounds Fun Network teams—Kelli, Emma, Jenna, Craig, Ashley, Heather, Cait, Chad. I love my job mostly because y'all are around. You each make these companies, and our office, so much better. Thank you.

To every guest on the *That Sounds Fun* podcast—you have taught me so much and brought joy to me and so many listeners. Thank you.

Baker Publishing Group—from dreaming around a dinner table in New York City, to the editing, designing, editing again, and marketing, this team is a dream to work with, and I'm so glad we're just getting started.

Lisa Jackson, I trust you with so many of my dreams, and you repeatedly make me glad I do. To many more. Thank you.

Matt Lehman, you have again designed a book cover that brings my stories to life in the most beautiful ways. I hope everyone judges this book by the cover. Thank you.

Shannan and Faitth, thank you for putting your wiser eyes on my work and teaching me what I didn't know. Very grateful for you both.

Pastor Kevin, Pastor Drew, Pastor Chris, the Cross Point Creative Team, and the whole Cross Point Church staff, I benefit so greatly from your teaching and leadership and how you serve our church and serve and love Jesus. Thank you.

Tony and Brooke and Lost Valley Ranch, you have become such a safe place for me. What you have built, and the friendship you offer, is sacred. Oooo-aaaah! Thank you.

David, you were very right when you said you've helped shape this book in a lot of ways. Fast isn't the kingdom. Thank you.

Helen, I mean this in the truest way—thanks so, so much. I miss you. And to Ashley and Betsy for your help that first weekend with the pup. It was no accident you were in town. Thank you.

Jenn and Rhett, I love you so. Your fingerprints and prayers are all over this one. Thank you.

Amber, you made our Dollywood dreams come true! Thank you.

My family and dearest friends, y'all are always better to me than I deserve, particularly when I'm neck deep in writing words for hours a day. Thank you for how you have learned me in this process and learned this process with me. I feel so safe on the hardest days of my work because my people understand. Thank you.

I ALSO FIND myself deeply missing my grandmothers lately, but I feel like they are close to me as I send my mind back to memories of the front porch and green beans and cathedral cookies. I'm thankful for how they both shaped my life and continue to do so.

In a strange way that has never happened before, having sports on the television while I've been writing has been incredibly helpful for this book in particular. So I'd like to thank the Atlanta Braves, the Atlanta Falcons, the Tennessee Titans, any and all college football teams (particularly the University of Georgia—Go, dawgs, sic 'em), European soccer clubs, Major League Soccer in the USA, and the Major League Baseball World Series for being the cadence to the rhythms of these pages.

I've also spent much time with the *Gilmore Girls* and on the Food Network channel and Hallmark Christmas movies as they played in the background of this book writing. It is such a strange grouping compared to my previous books that had very fancy music and a very bougie soundtrack. This has been baseball and Lorelai and Guy Fieri. That's what sounded fun to me. ☺

Finally, to Jesus, the author and perfecter of my faith. You have taught me the most, seen me at my worst, and loved me the hardest. I really love this life we've built. You saved me once, but You rescue me all the time. Every thank you is a thank you to You.

# Notes

### Ebenezer Road

1. J. R. R. Tolkien, *The Letters of J. R. R. Tolkien* (Boston: Houghton Mifflin, 1981), 109, https://www.goodreads.com/quotes/6730169-certainly -there-was-an-eden-on-this-very-unhappy-earth.

2. Webster's Third New International Dictionary, Unabridged, s.v. "abandon," accessed May 19, 2020, http://unabridged.merriam-webster .com.

### The Movie Theater

1. Dax Shepherd on his podcast, *Armchair Expert*, November 2, 2019, at the Tennessee Performing Arts Center in Nashville, TN.

### The High Line Hotel

1. Dictionary.com, s.v. "amateur," accessed May 21, 2020, https://www .dictionary.com/browse/amateur.

### *That Sounds Fun* Podcast Studio

1. This is my paraphrase of a famous quote by Wayne Gretzky.

### Disneyland

1. Jackie Gailey, "Disneyland Candlelight Processional Dates Confirmed December 7–8, 2019," Disney Information Station, October 11, 2019, https://www.wdwinfo.com/news-stories/disneyland-candlelight -processional-dates-confirmed-for-december-7-8-2019/.

### The Little White Kitchen

1. "Leftover Roast Chicken Soup with Roasted Vegetables," *Danielle Walker's Against All Grain* (blog), January 30, 2013, https://againstallgrain.com/2013/01/30/leftover-roast-chicken-soup-with-roasted-vegetables.

2. "1-Pot Pumpkin Black Bean Soup," *Minimalist Baker*, accessed May 19, 2020, https://minimalistbaker.com/1-pot-pumpkin-black-bean-soup/.

### The Pet Shop

1. Mwenya Mubanga et al., "Dog Ownership and the Risk of Cardiovascular Disease and Death—a Nationwide Cohort Study," *Scientific Reports* 7, no. 15821 (November 2017), https://doi.org/10.1038/s41598-017-16118-6.

### Sevier Park

1. *While You Were Sleeping*, directed by Jon Turteltaub; Burbank, CA: Hollywood Pictures, 1995.

### Neighbors Restaurant

1. Lexico Oxford Dictionary, s.v. "hobby," accessed May 21, 2020, https://www.lexico.com/en/definition/hobby.

**Annie F. Downs** is a bestselling author, sought-after speaker, and successful podcast host based in Nashville, Tennessee. Engaging and honest, she makes readers and listeners alike feel as if they've been longtime friends. Founder of the That Sounds Fun Network—which includes her aptly named flagship show, *That Sounds Fun*—and author of multiple bestselling books like *100 Days to Brave* and *Remember God*, Annie shoots straight and doesn't shy away from the tough topics. But she always finds her way back to the truth that God is good and that life is a gift. Annie is a huge fan of laughing with friends, confetti, soccer, and boiled peanuts (preferably from a backroads Georgia gas station).

Read more at **anniefdowns.com** and find her (embarrassingly easily) all over the internet **@anniefdowns**.

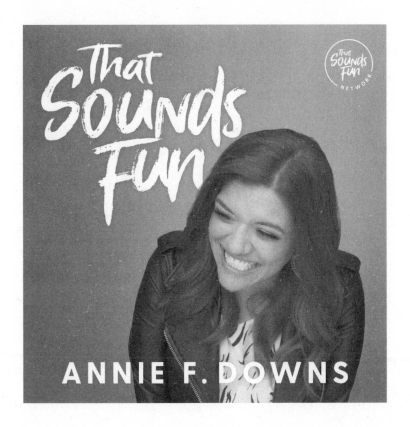

Less like a podcast and more like coffee with a friend, *That Sounds Fun*, Annie's podcast that releases on Mondays and Thursdays, features her favorite things and her favorite people. Pretty much, if it sounds fun to Annie, she wants you to hear about it!

Download or listen today
wherever you listen to podcasts!

# That Sounds Fun

## *children's book*

# by Annie F. Downs

## *coming fall 2021*

There are so many ways to have fun in this big, beautiful world. Annie shares some of her favorite ways to have fun in her debut children's book, and she wants to know . . .

**What sounds fun to YOU?**

waves roll at beach JACOB | Outdoor adventuring with my grand babies JEN | Coffee and a good making dance party with friends and coffee Laughter, comfort, love. across England KATHLEEN |

Coffee with good friends AMY | Time with my adult kids CATHY | Building friendships around a bonfire MANDY | Watching A quiet book-reading vacation AMY | Vacationing with nursing school friends AMBER | Making Rice Krispie treats HOLLY | with friends DANIELLE | Traveling to somewhere new TINA | Adventuring with my closest friends RUTH ANNE | Cuddling TERRI | The beach w/ my whole family JOCIE | Snuggling my husband and baby ALEX | Laughing with hubby & grown kids book MELISSA | Doing LIFE with my Eddie BROOKE | Drinking coffee and reading KARIS | Reading on a beach OLIVIA | Dinner JUSTINE | Making dinner for my friends RACHEL CLAIRE | Deep, transparent conversations with friends SEDONA | Laughing LINDSEY | Amusement park with friends LAUREN | Hiking with my dog JANA | Using the library hold system TAYLOR | Family together. BETHANY | Spending time with family, friends LISA | Mountain weekend with my husband KATIE | Reading in my PJs HOLLY | A walking tour Codirecting a musical SHURREE | Late night Waffle House KAI | Rescuing all the dogs CHERYL | Kayaking the Caney with friends KERSTYN | Road trip with crazy friends NICHOLE | Friends around my table ANDREA | Coffee. Friends. Reading. Date night. MADISON | Slow run on a Saturday CHRISTINA | Hiking in Yosemite KRISTEN | Jesus. Coffee. Friends. Date night. MADISON | Running with my dogs SARAH | Playing Yahtzee with my friends JILL | Beach vacation with my family ALYSSA | Crafting time with my sister AMY | Hearing my family's laughter EMILY | Traveling to the Netherlands LAURA | Romantic stroll through grocery store MICHELLE | Beach walking with Winston CAITLIN | Spending time with my family MORGAN | Sibling reunion with my favorites MELISSA | Hiking with family KRISTEN | Movie watching with my cat TAYLOR | Having our eleventh annual Thankmas AMORY | Camping by the lake LINDSAY | The mountains LEANNE | Being with my people AMBER | Exploring the outdoors with friends BETHANY | Road trips with best friends KATIE | Having Bible study with friends NICOLE | Going to see Hamilton. Again. RACHEL | Weekend away with my husband KIMBERLY | Spending time at the lake EMILY | Reading by a cozy fire MARY JANE | Beach, hubby, pooch, book, chocolate JENNIFER | Celebrating life with friends JULIANNE | Enjoying quality time with family JODIE | Time with my dogs outside KELLY | Christmas in New York City JESSICA | Book, iced tea, sunshine–simultaneously :) LAURIE | Framily trips after all babies AMORY | Belly laughs with my nieces BETHANY (AUNT B) | Planting flowers in the spring CASSIE | Minute to Win It party JILL | Family + friends + faith + food = fun LAUREN | Getting lost in the woods BRANDY | Stepping foot on every continent JENNA | Watching football with my nephew JENNABETH | Drinking coffee with my friends AMBRI | Drinking iced coffee with friends KATIE | First Christmas with my boys KATY | Celebrating anything with my family KATIE | Early morning family dance parties DELANEY | Neighborhood walks, peppermint hot chocolate GRACE | Fun with family and friends TAYLOR | Adopting my baby girl RACHEL | Sunny lake days with friends KARI | Walking on beach with friends MICHELLE | Best friends, no time constraints LISA | Being the woman He called BRANDI | Hiking with my dog RENEE | Beach date with my BFF KIM | Travel internationally with my BFFs JANE | Falling in love MELISSA | Hallmark movie bingo with friends MAGGIE | Playing board games with family AMY | Lots of coffee and books ANDY | Falling in love MELISSA | Adventuring with my husband ASHLEY | My team winning it all LIZZIE | Family time in the mountains COURTNEY | Jesus, coffee, mountains, family CHRISTY | Movie day with my husband ANNA-LISA | Sharing Disney with my family DEONNA | Laughing with people KATIE | Teaching little, yet capable minds JENNY | Campfire chats in the mountains ANNA-LISA | Concert with my fiancé LEXI | Buffalo chicken dip & Alabama football KATIE | Reading Watching Hallmark movies all day ANNA | Running/finishing my first ultramarathon GRETCHEN | Game night with friends EMILY | Cheer on IU basketball NATALIE | Reading books on the beach KRISTEN | Vacation with my favorite people ALEXA | Doing life with my PEOPLE LYNZI | Horseback riding STEPHANIE | Winter cabin trip with friends EMILY | Camping and boating LAURA | Reading next to a fire RACHEL | Being with my family LYDIA | Dreaming about what is next BB | Hammocking with my family EMILEE | Booking a spontaneous trip MIKAYLA | Reading, wine, music, blanket, fire MELISSA | Calling the Hogs in November LAWSON | Watching sunsets MJOY | Loving my people EMILEE | Sabbath day and artsy journal CAROL | Visiting Disney World with family KARA | Hot cocoa and a good book STEPHANIE | Movie nights with aging parents CARINA | Backpacking throughout the West Coast KARLY | Setting a beautiful table MARTHA | Mountaineering with my dog ASHLEIGH | Kayaking during a Minnesota sunset COLLEEN |

Breakfast foods w/ framily ANYTIME | Game-day reporter for Philadelphia Eagles LIV | Tea and a good book JACLYN | Bubble bath with a book RACHEL | Deep fireside chats with friends EMILY | Filling my home with laughter JANNAH | Hanging with family in Aggieland BRANDY | Sledding with my friends BECKY | Deep conversations with friends SYDNEY | A spontaneous day trip WHITNEY | Trip to Nashville & concert MIA | Being creative with cross-stitch AMBER | Traveling to Hallmark movie locations MARSHA | Road trips and mountain climbing HOLLY | Walt Disney World KAITLYN | Opening a speech therapy clinic KATELYNN | Tex-Mex with friends TINA | Coffee in the great outdoors REBECCA | Shopping with my friend Maddie EMILY | Coffee with my friend Lisa ALISON | Watching Hallmark Christmas movies all year HEATHER | Vacations with my best friend SARAH | Beach ANYTIME OF YEAR SHEA | Spending time with my husband REBEKAH | Being outside all day LORA | Traveling with my new husband KRISSY | Traveling with my husband AMY | Starting a baking podcast JEN | Long weekends at the shore AMY | Going for fancy high tea LAURA | Exploring a new city KRISTEN | Being with my best friends MEGAN | Going to Disney on Christmas SARA | Snuggling with my dogs BETHANY | Reading a great book ASHLEY | All the concerts with friends AIMEE | Road trip adventure with friends MARILLYN | A trip with my people KAMI | Eating lobster-foil meals beachside TAMMY | Spending time with my husband BETHANY | Setting up a Christmas tree MIGUEL | Being outside with my people EMILY | Coffee and early morning hiking MARILLYN | Spending time with my husband JULIANNA | Traveling with my family DAKOTA | Starting my new job STEPHANIE | Figuring out my passion STEPHANIE | Dancing with friends all night KRISTEN | Seeing the sunrise in Hawaii KERIE | A road trip with friends MEGAN | Summer reading on my deck LAURA | Cabin trip with whole family MELISSA | Creation, friends, music, road trip KRISTEN | A reading vacation DEB | Hot chocolate JENNA | Going skydiving HANNAH | Half-birthday surprise parties GRACE | Beach trip, my people & food JEN | Skiing in fresh powder MORIAH | WRITE AMY | Hot chocolate with friends LAURA | Hanging with my people KELLY | Colorful trail running during fall MELISSA | College football game and winning KAILEY | Spontaneous adventures + genuine convos AFTIN | A Christmas market in Germany RACHEL | A week at Disney World KELLY | Snow skiing with my family STACI | Performing the Bach Cello Suites KATHLEEN | Spa day by the ocean LAUREN | Eating a churro at Disneyland ALEXANDRA | Beach. Books. Coffee. Friends. MIKAELA | Smoky Mountains in the fall MELISSA | Baking for people I love ANNALISE | Traveling the world, living overseas MACKENZIE | Snowboarding in remote mountains JEN | Reading on the cabin porch STEENIE | High tea with the Queen KRISTEN | Raising kids in Edinburgh, Scotland LIZZIE | A reading vacation DEB | Mountain cabin fireplace with family MARLEETA | Traveling the WORLD AMY | Playing trivia with my family CHRISTI | Reading in a hammock KELLIE | Hanging out with friends STEPHANIE | Year-round Christmas trees ASHLIE | Beach trip with my coonhound ALÉ | Nephews greeting me at airport JENNIFER | Watching a rom-com with girlfriends BETSY | Painting and writing ABIGAIL | Margaritas on the beach CARA | Sharing my art with others CARYS | Beach, drinking margaritas, eating guacamole DANA | Our people together off-grid HEATHER | Meeting our Esmé Lylah girl CHARLISE | My people together around food HEATHER | Being with my cats ANDRIA | Saturday pancakes with my family MEG | I coach high school volleyball KENDRA | Relaxing with hubby and puppy EMILY | Playing with my dog ALAINA | Wedding feast with my people HEATHER | Watching Alabama football in Tuscaloosa LAURA | Unlimited first-class airline tickets TORI | Being home in Ireland EMMA | Adventuring around the world ALLISON | Spending time with my kids SHANNON | Golfing on a beautiful day COURTNEY | Weekend outside with family SARAH | Playing football with my brothers JAMISON | Pun parties with best friends ANDY | Hanging with Mike and Cameron WENDY | Meeting our daughter next year JESSICA | Yoga + coffee with a friend GABRIELLE | An adventure with my husband CATHY | Country concert outside in Colorado with friends ANNA | Roller coasters at Dollywood PAYSIE | Dance party with my son RACHEL | Playing football with my people ASHLEY | Relaxing with a good book SUE | Time with my best people ALEX | Coffee dates and singing Broadway KRISTINA | Sleeping in and Bible recap IDA | Drinking coffee on my couch LEAH | Three-month holiday in Italy ELIZE | Coffee and a good book DEBBY | A sunny day at Disney ALLISON | String quartets, tea, and cats ANNAGRACE | Traveling to see friends ELIZABETH | Reading on the warm beach KENDAL | All things Disney AMY | Marry my best friend, Mark LAVON | Giving away money CATHY | Adventures with my family RACHEL | Time at the beach LEAH |